BOAT TRAILERS AND TOW VEHICLES
A USER'S GUIDE

DATE DUE

DEMCO, INC. 38-3012

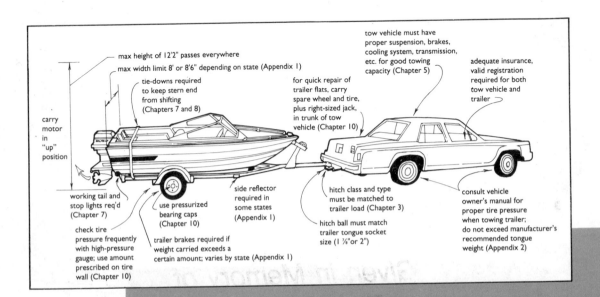

max height of 12'2" passes everywhere

max width limit 8' or 8'6" depending on state (Appendix 1)

tow vehicle must have proper suspension, brakes, cooling system, transmission, etc. for good towing capacity (Chapter 5)

adequate insurance, valid registration required for both tow vehicle and trailer

tie-downs required to keep stern end from shifting (Chapters 7 and 8)

for quick repair of trailer flats, carry spare wheel and tire, plus right-sized jack, in trunk of tow vehicle (Chapter 10)

carry motor in "up" position

working tail and stop lights req'd (Chapter 7)

use pressurized bearing caps (Chapter 10)

side reflector required in some states (Appendix 1)

hitch class and type must be matched to trailer load (Chapter 3)

consult vehicle owner's manual for proper tire pressure when towing trailer; do not exceed manufacturer's recommended tongue weight (Appendix 2)

check tire pressure frequently with high-pressure gauge; use amount prescribed on tire wall (Chapter 10)

trailer brakes required if weight carried exceeds a certain amount; varies by state (Appendix 1)

hitch ball must match trailer tongue socket size (1 ⅞"or 2")

BOAT TRAILERS AND TOW VEHICLES
A USER'S GUIDE

Steve Henkel

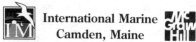

International Marine
Camden, Maine

International Marine/
Ragged Mountain Press
A Division of The McGraw-Hill Companies

10 9 8 7 6 5 4

Library of Congress Cataloging-in-Publication Data

Henkel, Steve.
    Boat trailers and tow vehicles / Steve Henkel.
        p.   cm.
    Includes index
    ISBN 0-87742-290-7
    1. Boat trailers.   1. Title
TL297.H45 1991   91-4511
629.225—dc20   CIP

Questions regarding the content of this book should be addressed to:

International Marine
P.O. Box 220
Camden, Maine 04843

Questions regarding the ordering of this book should be addressed to:

The McGraw-Hill Companies
Customer Service Department
P.O. Box 547
Blacklick, OH 43004
Retail customers: 1-800-822-8158
Bookstores: 1-800-722-4726

Typeset by High Resolution, Camden, ME
Printed by Quebecor Printing Co., Fairfield, PA
Design by Patrice M. Rossi
Illustrated by the author
Edited by Jonathan Eaton
Production by Janet Robbins

CONTENTS

Acknowledgments

Writing a book like *Boat Trailers and Tow Vehicles* requires help from many sources. Of particular value was advice and information obtained from: the research staff at the Darien Public Library, namely Maura Ritz, Blanche Parker, and Sarah Polirer; Mario Orro and Steve Mathis at Triad Trailer; Fred Fuest at Pirelli-Armstrong Tire Co.; Clarence Ericson at Dico; Greg Smith and Kent Gabrys at U-Haul; Dave Ronchetto at Shoreline Products; Scott Johnston at Wesbar Corp.; Robert Mayer at Cole-Hersee Co.; and Richard Brooks at Brooks Sales & Engineering. To these folks I extend a special measure of thanks for their time and effort above and beyond the call of duty.

My appreciation also goes to the literally hundreds of representatives of trailer builders, accessory suppliers, and tow vehicle manufacturers who contributed brochures, specifications, and other valuable materials to the information base from which this book was created.

To Jon Eaton, Molly Mulhern, and the rest of the staff at International Marine Publishing I offer my thanks for seeing that *Boat Trailers and Tow Vehicles* got out of manuscript and into print in a highly refined yet timely manner.

Finally to Carol, my wife, as always, I give my love and appreciation for her unswerving encouragement and patience.

Preface

Over the years since 1961, when I built my first boat trailer from a bolt-together kit, I have accumulated a tremendous amount of experience while making a tremendous number of mistakes. Although these mistakes seem to have covered an impressively wide swath of endeavors both inside and outside the marine field, many of my more memorable errors are directly associated with various aspects of boat trailering.

For example, I have lost many pieces and parts of expensive marine equipment along the highway while trailering because it didn't occur to me to screw, tape, or tie them down securely enough. I have suffered the embarrassment of a collapsed trailer axle in the middle of a busy intersection because I didn't think to inspect the trailer's structure periodically, and didn't have a clear idea of what to inspect or how to go about it. I have crept painfully up hill and down dale trying to pull a boat on a trailer with a tow vehicle that just didn't have the power to do the job. I have waded up to my waist in icy cold water because I didn't know the proper way to launch and retrieve a boat on a shallow ramp. I have damaged an outboard motor skeg and ruined a propeller through inept boat-trailer handling on the ramp. I have sweated for hours to make my trailer lights work, blowing fuses and making a rat's nest of wires when there was no circuit diagram to point the way to a successful repair. And I have suffered other excruciating embarrassments too horrible to describe.

All these problems could have been avoided if I had read a book — this book, or one like it. But unfortunately, until now, there has been no single volume on the market that covered the whole territory of choosing, using, maintaining and repairing a boat trailer, and selecting and equipping the right tow vehicle.

It was, it seemed to me, quite remarkable that there is this gap in the literature, considering that there are something like 5,000,000 boat trailers in use right now, and roughly 200,000 new ones coming into service every year. And so it is that I decided to write this book — for the millions of owners and users of boat trailers who are, as I once was, learning the art of trailering largely from their own mistakes. Now, finally, they have a better alternative: Read this book.

Steve Henkel
Darien, Connecticut
August 28, 1990

How to Choose
the Right Trailer

CHAPTER ONE.

The Pluses and Minuses of Boat Trailering

Trailering is fun, and today it's simple to do once you know how. If you match the right trailer to your boat and the right tow vehicle to your trailer, you can tow with ease. In fact, with the right equipment you'll hardly know there's a load behind you, and launching and retrieving will be a breeze.

Advantages of Buying a Trailer

Having your own boat trailer provides many benefits. There is the economic benefit of not having to pay the marina for dock space or for launching and pulling out your boat. With prices for slips running at over $100 per foot of boat length for a three-month season in some parts of the country and marina service costs rising proportionately, that's a significant plus.

There is also the added convenience of being able to store your boat in your own garage or backyard, where she's easy to admire and to work on whenever you get the urge. Maintenance is reduced, algae and barnacles won't accumulate on the hull, and there's less chance of corrosion of metal parts.

Best of all, acquiring a trailer for your boat can open vast new territories — literally thousands of miles of lakes and coastline — for you to explore by land and sea. You'll have the added flexibility of being able to travel to the best cruising grounds, waterski areas, fishing holes, or regatta sites without lengthy on-the-water treks. That freedom — to travel where you want, when you want — is the secret of trailering success. It goes a long way to explain why today there are some 5,000,000 boats trailers in use in the USA alone, with some 200,000 new ones entering the U.S. market each year.

Disadvantages of Buying

Of course, every story has two sides. The disadvantages of owning your own trailer start with having to pay a significant up-front purchase cost — anywhere from a couple of hundred dollars to several thousand. Then there is the vehicle registration to be renewed each year, the insurance premiums, the parking space required, the maintenance to be dealt with, the gradual depreciation in value. . . . The list goes on.

Perhaps the biggest potential disadvantage of owning your own boat trailer is the need for a proper tow vehicle. Your present vehicle may or may not be suitable, but you should be aware that any boat bigger than a Sunfish or a canoe will need a vehicle with a specific towing capacity rated by its manufacturer. In these days of auto "down-sizing," lighter weight, front-wheel drive, and unitized bodies, your vehicle's rated capacity may be too low to pull your boat. (Appendix 2 lists capacities for most 1991 vehicle models.) Many people, even those who have been trailering boats for years, don't realize that more than two-thirds of all new cars, passenger vans, and sports utility vehicles (SUVs) cannot tow a combined load over 2,000 pounds, including boat, trailer, passengers, and gear.

Surprising? Perhaps not, until you realize that 2,000 pounds happens to be the weight of an average 17-foot runabout and trailer loaded with a modest amount of gear — and 17 feet isn't very big, as trailerable boats go.

This book is mostly about the ready-to-roll variety of boat trailers. Nevertheless, if you're not sure you want to buy a ready-made trailer and are looking for alternatives, here are some ideas.

• Use a cartop carrier, a dolly, or both. Cartop carriers generally aren't used for loads over 100 to 150 pounds per crossbar, not only because it's hard to hoist a heavier boat to roof height, but also because the sheet metal and rain gutters of today's vehicles aren't made to support much weight. If you doubt it, try pushing the heel of your hand into the roof of your car (but be careful not to push so hard that you damage the sheet metal). You'll find that with most cars, even near the roof edge there's too little strength to support a big load.

Consequently it's best to limit the weight of cartop boats to 150 pounds or so, and check carrier manufacturer specs on load-carrying capacity before buying.

Hand-pulled dollies such as the Carrello Cart pictured in Figure 1-1 — or its near-clone, the Rolec Dinghy Dolly — are good for launching and dry-storing

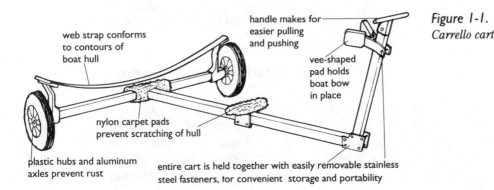

web strap conforms
to contours of
boat hull

handle makes for
easier pulling
and pushing

vee-shaped
pad holds
boat bow
in place

nylon carpet pads
prevent scratching of hull

plastic hubs and aluminum
axles prevent rust

entire cart is held together with easily removable stainless
steel fasteners, for convenient storage and portability

Figure 1-1.
Carrello cart

cartoppable boats and other lightweight small craft up to 200 pounds or so. But watch out for hull "dimples" that can develop on lightly built craft where some dolly supports poke into thin areas of the skin. And don't try pulling a dolly behind your car on the road; it's illegal and dangerous. Don't laugh; I've seen it tried.

• Rent or borrow a trailer. You can try renting or borrowing, but you're likely to have problems finding a trailer this way. First of all, even if you find one with the right rated capacity, adjusting the trailer to fit the boat (see Chapter 7) is sometimes a lengthy process that even your best friend, let alone a rental agent, might be reluctant to undertake. Second, it's easy for an uninformed user to abuse a boat trailer to the point that costly repairs are needed, so again, owners might be hesitant to entrust their trailers to you.

For these and other reasons, not many rental services offer boat trailers, but you might find one if you're persistent. To test that theory, I recently called a dozen rental service companies and boat trailer dealers in my area, and found only a single establishment with a single trailer — an EZ Loader with a capacity of 19 feet or 1,900 pounds. It rented for $14 an hour with a minimum of 3 hours ($14 x 3 = $42), and the rental agreement stipulated use within a 15-mile radius of the renter. Not bad if you plan to use a trailer once or twice a year locally, but impractical if you want to take your boat away on a vacation for a weekend or longer.

• Build from a kit. Examine a number of boat trailers and you'll see that many of them are put together mostly with nuts and bolts. If you're handy with tools, you may be able to assemble a trailer from a kit and save money in the process. Some trailer dealers and quite a few mail-order houses — Sears Roebuck for example — offer assemble-it-yourself kits. Figure 1-2 shows the pieces of a Sears trailer for 10- to 14-foot boats. Check your local dealer or the suppliers listed in Appendix 3 for more details on kit trailers.

Figure 1-2.
Sears, Roebuck trailer kit

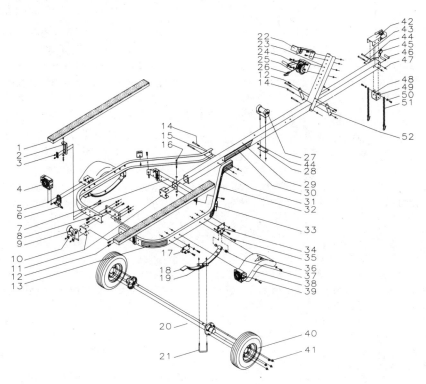

SEARS BOAT TRAILER
371.619800, 371.619911

KEY NO	PART NO	DESCRIPTION	QTY REQ'D	KEY NO	PART NO	DESCRIPTION	QTY REQ'D
1	15-40117	Bol Asy 2x4x5 Flt W/hdwe	2	27	14-60165	5" N.A. Molded K/R Assembly	1
2	21-00999	Bol Brkt Lg TF17 Galv	4	28	21-00027	Spacer Tilt Latch 2x4-1/2 11GA	1
3	30-26740	Nut Hex Free 3/8-16 ZP	10	29	21-17035	Tng 3x3x10-CLSI(1/2" Blt) TE14	1
4	30-55306	T/L Sub LH 8-way Peterson	1	30	17-80102	Tape Sears 21" RH	1
5	30-26345	Scrw Trs Slt Mchn 1/4-20x3/4 ZP	1	31	17-80103	Tape Sears 10" Square	2
6	30-55314	License Plate Bracket Peterson	1	32	30-63242	Decal GMFSHR Blk 1.5/8x14.1/2	2
7	21-15001	Crossmember TE14 Slid Tng	1	33	30-55300	S/M C/L Amb Submer Peterson	2
8	21-02030	Splicer 4x9 MGLV TE14, TE16	1	34	13-80310	Spring Hanger Brkt Assy PLTD	2
9	14-60030	4" Keel Roller & Adj Brkt	1	35	30-25611	Bolt Hex 1/2-13x3.1/4 G5 ZP	2
10	30-27100	Washer Pyramidal 3/8 ZP	10	36	21-09899	Brkt Fnd TE 2x4 10Ga	2
11	21-02032	Bracket F/Sliding Tongue	1	37	30-18251	Bushing Spring F/SE Single Axle	4
12	30-25280	Bolt Hex 3/8-16x1 ZP	36	38	17-00007	Fndr 8" TE14 7x19x22 MGLV	2
13	17-80100	Tape Sears 14" Square	4	39	30-55307	T/L Submer RH 7-way Peterson	1
14	30-25280	Bolt Hex 3/8-16x3.3/4 ZP	6	40	30-20270	T&W 480x8A 5-Lug Std Wheel	2
15	11-10100	FRM SD TE14 MGLV	2	41	30-21091	Lug Nut 1/2x13.1/16" Hex ZP	10
16	30-25290	Bolt Hex 3/8-16x4 ZP	1	42	17-72018	Cplr Kit 1.7/8 Pltd 1/2 Blt 3x3	1
17	13-80311	Spring Glide Brkt Assy Plated	2	43	30-25640	Bolt Hex 1/2-13x4 ZP	2
18	30-53000	Spring 2 Leaf 24" SE .262G 600#	2	44	30-18280	Grommet 1/8x3/8 ID x 5/8 OD	2
19	21-00001	Spr Clmp 3 HL SM 1.5x4.25x.25	2	45	17-50005	Wir Harness Kit Wishbone 17'	1
20	13-00471	Axle Asy 44" W/3/4	1	46	21-04010	Inner Tongue Spacer, 5x2.25	2
21	30-26630	U-Bolt 1/2x2.9/16x4 SQ ZP	2	47	30-26850	Nut Hex Lock 1/2-13 CP	6
22	14-10010	B/S 8" W/V	1	48	30-26830	Nut Hex Lock 3/8-16 CP	33
23	21-01103	W/S 18" - 8.1/2x25.3/8 MGLV	1	49	21-17070	Tng Knee 2x9 Pltd	1
24	30-51360	Winch DL-600 or Fulton T-600	1	50	30-27020	Washer Flat 3/8 ZP	26
25	21-07000	Rope 5/16 x 16 FT	1	51	21-00006	Chain Assembly 3/16" x 16 Link	2
26	32-62140	Hook 3000# CLSD Laclede	1	52	21-00006	W/S Brace Small 1.1/4x8	2
				53	17-80101	Tape Sears 21" LH	1

• Build your own design from scratch. If you know how to weld, have access to both welding equipment and small quantities of rectangular tubing and structural steel shapes at large-quantity prices, have studied the motor vehicle laws of your state as to inspection and registration requirements for home-built trailers, know enough about trailer design to create a safe and roadworthy vehicle, and have the time and patience to do the job right, you may be someone who can build a trailer and be happy with the result. If so, you're a rare breed; most homemade trailers turn out to be useless junk.

If you decide to build your own despite the above caveats, at least one company specializes in supplying many of the pieces and parts you'll need. Last time I checked, they were glad to send a free catalog for the asking, and were even willing to discuss your building problems and give needed advice over the phone. The place is Trailer Parts International, Inc., 8110 NW 56th St., Miami FL 33152. For advice, call 305-592-1879, or to order parts or a catalog, call toll free, 800-346-6909. If you need help with basic design, GLEN-L Marine Designs sells "How To Build Boat Trailers" for the modest price (in 1990) of $8.95 (Box 1804, Bellflower, CA 90706; 213-630-6258).

Certain homemade trailers don't require welding. But some of these designs, such as the wood-framed structure shown in Figure 1-3, may not be suitable for highway use.

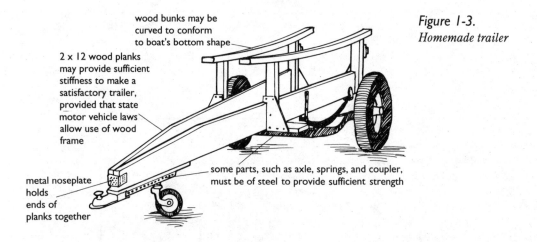

wood bunks may be
curved to conform
to boat's bottom shape

2 x 12 wood planks
may provide sufficient
stiffness to make a
satisfactory trailer,
provided that state
motor vehicle laws
allow use of wood
frame

metal noseplate
holds
ends of
planks together

some parts, such as axle, springs, and coupler,
must be of steel to provide sufficient strength

Figure 1-3.
Homemade trailer

If after considering all the angles you decide to buy a ready-made boat trailer rather than pursue any of the above alternatives, you'll need to know where to look, what to look for, and how much to budget for your new purchase. The rest of Part One is devoted to helping you sort out answers to these questions.

CHAPTER TWO

Prices and Sources of Supply

O nce you've decided that you want to buy a trailer, one of the first questions to be answered is whether to buy new or used. As you'll see below, the two choices bring with them significant differences in price as well as other factors.

If you're shopping for a boat, new or used, you'll find many being sold with trailer. In those cases you'll want to appraise the value of the trailer as well as the boat.

Then, if money is an object, as it is for most of us, you'll probably want to know what continuing costs you face after you buy your trailer. You'll find useful indicators on that subject in this chapter.

Finally, assuming you already own a boat and are shopping only for a trailer, you'll want to develop a feel for what's available locally that might fit your needs. This chapter outlines where to look.

Buying New Versus Used

There are two ways to buy a ready-made trailer: new and used. If you buy new, you can be reasonably certain that the wheel bearings aren't about to burn out, rust hasn't penetrated the frame in hidden nooks and crannies, the wiring and lights are in good working order . . . and if problems surface, you can ask your friendly dealer to help you solve them without fear of being rebuffed (at least in most cases).

Used trailers are unlikely to offer any of these advantages, especially if you're not quite sure how to conduct a detailed inspection. But used trailers are almost always significantly less costly — and after reading this book you'll be prepared to judge the relative soundness of any trailer, enabling you to buy with confidence whether you opt for used or new.

Prices

To give you an idea of how much boat trailers cost new, Figure 2-1 offers a sample of typical prices, gleaned from recent ads in the northeastern U.S. Prices in other parts of the country may vary somewhat, depending among other things on distance from factory to market and on how much competition exists locally.

Figure 2-1.
Prices of new boat trailers

Trailer Capacity in Terms of —			Trailer Capacity in Terms of —		
Boat Length (feet)	Boat Weight (pounds)	Typical Range of New Trailer Prices	Boat Length (feet)	Boat Weight (pounds)	Typical Range of New Trailer Prices
10-13	200	$250 to 350	11-14	400	$275 to 450
12-15	600	300 to 500	13-16	800	350 to 550
14-17	1,200	450 to 650	15-18	1,500	650 to 950
16-19	1,750	700 to 1,100	17-20	2,000	750 to 1,200
18-21	2,300	1,000 to 1,400	19-22	2,550	1,200 to 1,500
19-22	2,950	1,450 to 2,100	19-23	3,500	1,800 to 2,600
19-24	4,400	2,200 to 3,000	20-25	5,000	2,600 to 3,600
21-26	5,400	3,000 to 4,000	21-27	6,000	3,500 to 4,500
23-28	7,000	4,000 to 5,000	25-29	8,000	4,500 to 5,500
26-30	9,000	5,000 to 6,000	27-31	10,000	5,500 to 7,000
28-32	11,000	6,000 to 8,000	29-33	12,000	7,000 to 10,000
30-34	14,400	8,000 to 12,000	30-35	15,500	10,000 to 14,000
31-36	17,000	12,000 to 16,000			

Notes: Exact prices depend on several factors, including but not limited to:

• whether trailer bed is bunk or roller type (bunk is less expensive);

• whether painted or galvanized (painted is less);

• whether brakes are installed (figure on adding around $400 for one axle or $600 for two axles if capacity is less than about 4,600 pounds, ranging up to around $550 for one axle or $750 for two axles if capacity is over 6,000 pounds).

• whether competition is heavy or light. Discounted prices are common wherever competition among local trailer vendors is present, as are seasonal sales (usually in the fall and spring).

If you buy used instead of new, you can expect to pay roughly 10 to 90% less than the above prices, depending — just as for cars — on the model, age, and condition of the trailer. Figure 2-2 presents some used trailer price guidelines to help you evaluate "deals."

Figure 2-2.
Guidelines for used trailer prices

Age of Trailer in Years	Percentage of New (Discounted) Price		
	Better-than-Average Condition	Average Condition	Worse-than-Average Condition
0 (new)	100%	100%	100%
1	92	88	83
2	82	78	73
3	75	70	64
4	68	63	56
5	62	56	49
6	55	49	42
7	51	44	36
8	46	39	31
9	43	35	26
10	39	31	22
11	37	28	18
12	34	25	15
13	32	22	12
14	30	20	10
15 or more	28	18	10 or less

Other Costs

In planning your trailering budget, it's well to remember that there are other costs in addition to the trailer itself. For example, there are the costs of insurance premiums, maintenance, storage, and equipping your tow vehicle with the proper trailer hitch and associated equipment. Here's what to expect.

Insurance

Premiums for trailer coverage take two forms: trailer damage and liability. Rates vary from company to company, but generally the carrier that insures your boat will insure the trailer at a very modest additional premium. For example, I pay a rate of only 2½% of valuation per year for $100 deductible property coverage on my fleet of trailers, as part of my "Aquamaster" CNA Insurance Company boat policies. That works out to only $12.50 a year for a trailer valued at $500. Liability insurance for on-the-road accidents is included at no extra cost — and is covered by my auto policy as well.

Maintenance

Boat trailers suffer a lot of wear and tear not associated with other types of over-the-road vehicles, primarily as a result of submersion at launching ramps. If you can avoid dunking your trailer (by using a hoist or crane to lift your boat between water and trailer, for instance), your trailer maintenance will be infinitely easier. You won't have to regrease the wheel hubs as often. You won't have to touch up scratches in the paint or galvanizing as frequently, or repair the lighting circuit as often. And that generally means you'll pay significantly less for maintenance. Some typical costs for these jobs and other periodic trailer maintenance requirements are given in Figure 2-3.

Figure 2-3.
Typical trailer maintenance costs

Maintenance Item	Labor Cost (see note) Hours	$	Material Cost	Total Cost
Remove and repack one pair of wheel hubs	1.5	$ 60	$ 2	$ 62
Sand and repaint trailer body	8	320	25	345
Replace wiring and lights	2	80	30	110
Replace worn tire	Incl.	Incl.	35	35
Replace tube only	Incl.	Incl.	10	10

Note: Labor cost is assumed to be $40 per hour. Actual cost may vary considerably from one locality to another.

Storage

Costs for seasonal storage vary from nothing (if you keep your trailer in your backyard) to fees in the high two-figure range per foot of boat length per year in places frequented by the carriage trade. If you're planning to store your boat — or your empty trailer — at a boatyard or other commercial facility, you can avoid nasty surprises by checking local prices before deciding which facility to use.

Towing Equipment

Costs for properly equipping your tow vehicle can add up, too. To analyze these costs, let's start with the hitch.

Except in the case of very large trailers pulled by trucks (which are beyond the scope of this book), boat trailers must be towed by a vehicle equipped with a tow ball mounted on a bar that is solidly connected to the vehicle's frame. Except for the step bumpers sometimes used on pickup trucks, bumper hitches used in the past are no longer suitable for today's shock-absorbing bumpers. Even U-Haul, the world's largest hitch installer with 1,100 company-owned installation centers plus a network of over 3,500 independent dealers, will only mount rental-type bumper hitches on cars to pull U-Haul-rented lightweight utility trailers. Generally they won't rent them separately or allow their use on boat trailers.

U-Haul does, however, encourage the installation of permanent hitches. Their installed prices as this edition is written (in the autumn of 1990) vary with the size of the hitch, the complexity of the installation, and the cost of labor in a particular geographical area. For example, labor costs vary from $25 to $50 an hour or more; installation time can take anywhere from ½ hour for a simple Class I hitch to almost two hours for a complicated job; and hitch prices vary all the way from $36 for the simplest Class I hitch to $183 for a big Class III hitch. (See Figure 3-4 for the definitions of these classes.) The net effect of all this is that installed hitch prices range from $50 or $60 for a simple Class I job to almost $300 for a big, complicated one.

In addition to the hitch itself (which in U-Haul's case includes installation of lighting wiring), you may need other items if they're not already installed on your tow vehicle. These include a heavy-duty flasher ($6 to $12), extended-arm rearview mirrors for seeing around the sides of wide trailers ($10 to $60), and perhaps most important (and most expensive), a trailer towing package, needed on most vehicles if you plan to tow loads greater than a couple of thousand pounds. What's in a tow package can vary; see Chapter 5 for details. Tow packages cost from nothing — if, say, a tow package comes standard on a new car — to $2,000 or more for a complex retrofit job.

Depreciation and Life Expectancy

Many boaters ignore maintenance on their trailers and after a few years begin to have major problems, especially with frame and axle corrosion and wheel bearing failures. These folks probably figure that the life expectancy of a trailer they own is four or five years, and they're close to right. But if a program of faithful maintenance is followed (as outlined in Chapters 10, 11, and 12), a well-built and properly used trailer can last 20 to 30 years or even longer. The moral of the story is to pay attention to scheduled preventive maintenance. By doing so you can save thousands of dollars over a period of years.

If you need an incentive to think seriously about maintenance, figure it this way: Annual depreciation on a $2,000 trailer you replace every 5 years is $400, whereas annual depreciation on the same trailer junked after 25 years is only $80 a year — a saving of $320 a year, or roughly $8,000 over 25 years. And if you figure new trailer prices are constantly rising over the 25 years, and that you can earn interest every year on the money you save, the real saving is considerably more.

Where to Find Boat Trailers for Sale

For sources of new trailers, try the telephone book Yellow Pages, scan regional boating periodicals such as *Soundings* and *Latitude 38* for ads, or write direct to trailer manufacturers. A list of more than 40 manufacturing companies appears in Appendix 3. For used trailers, your local classified ads will be the best source of leads. Boat and boat trailer dealers may occasionally offer "pre-owned" trailers or demos for sale as well.

CHAPTER THREE

Finding the Right Trailer

Finding the right trailer to fit your boat usually isn't a simple job. If you're buying new, you can entrust the task to your friendly trailer dealer — but he probably only stocks one or two brands and may be tempted to try "force fitting" an unsuitable trailer he has in stock to your boat and your needs.

Alternatively, you can query other boat owners with craft similar to yours, find out which make and model of trailer they find most satisfactory, and buy that type. Of course, you'll then have to accept their opinions as to what is "satisfactory" — and to many boat owners who have never owned the right trailer for their vessel, ignorance is bliss.

The third — and best — choice is to figure out for yourself which trailer is best for you and your boat, using the guidelines in this chapter. Then, even if you end up asking a trailer dealer for recommendations, you'll know from his answers whether he's a straight shooter. Not that most trailer dealers aren't. But the educated consumer is likely to get the best results.

Picking the Right Type: Bunk Type, Roller Type, or Flatbed?

"Bunk"-type or "float-on" trailers (Figure 3-1) have rails or "bunks," usually carpet-covered, from which the boat hull can be floated or slid on and off. They're suitable for well-designed steep launching ramps on which the trailer can be immersed all the way up to the top of its fenders. At that point shallow-draft boats can be floated off, and deeper-draft boats can usually be slid off if given a guide bars (also called "positioning poles") at sides of some bunk-type trailers give visual indicator of how to position boat

bunks, usually of carpet-padded wood but sometimes of steel - and sometimes with rollers along top edge - are also called bunkers, bolsters, or bolster boards

Figure 3-1.
Bunk-type trailer

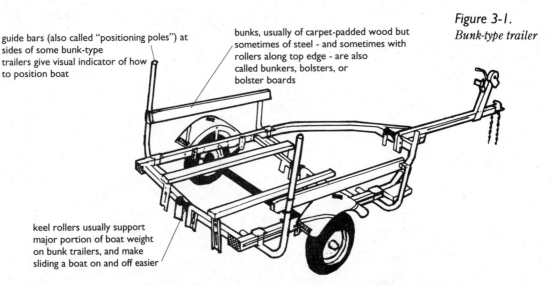

keel rollers usually support major portion of boat weight on bunk trailers, and make sliding a boat on and off easier

little nudge at the bow. The main advantages of bunk-type trailers are: (1) on average they are less expensive than the roller type, and (2) continuous fore-and-aft hull support can usually be arranged by judicious adjustment of the bunk positions, so that the hull is at minimum risk of damage from jounces and jolts on the road.

"Roller"-type or "roll-on" trailers (Figure 3-2) use low-friction rubber-faced or plastic rollers on adjustable brackets to make boat launching and retrieval easier. Since the boat moves on and off easier on rollers than skids, roller-type trailers often can be used on ramps that aren't steep enough for a bunk-type trailer. Moreover, on steep ramps it's often easier to winch a heavy boat onto a set of rollers than to skid her onto bunks. But considerable extra hardware is involved, so the price of a roller-type trailer is typically 15 to 30% higher than that of a bunk-type trailer.

Flatbed trailers (Figure 3-3) are occasionally used to haul boats. Usually in this case the boat is supported by a firmly anchored but detachable cradle, which when removed permits the trailer to be used conveniently as a general carryall. But a flatbed trailer supports a boat relatively high off the ground and thus is often unusable on a launching ramp; instead, the boat and its cradle must be hoisted off with a crane or skidded off at the water's edge at low tide and secured until the incoming flood floats the boat off the cradle. In this case, the cradle and boat must be anchored separately, and provision must be made to prevent the cradle, if of wood or other buoyant material, from floating up against the bottom of the boat and thus preventing separation.

Some trailers can easily be converted from bunk-type to flatbed. You simply unbolt the bunks from their steel brackets. There are generally two or three

Figure 3-2.
Roller-type trailer

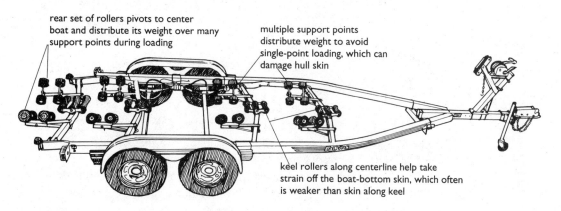

rear set of rollers pivots to center
boat and distribute its weight over many
support points during loading

multiple support points
distribute weight to avoid
single-point loading, which can
damage hull skin

keel rollers along centerline help take
strain off the boat-bottom skin, which often
is weaker than skin along keel

Figure 3-3.
Flatbed trailer

surface of planks or plywood can
be built over existing trailer frame
to accommodate non-boating needs
or to carry a boat cradle

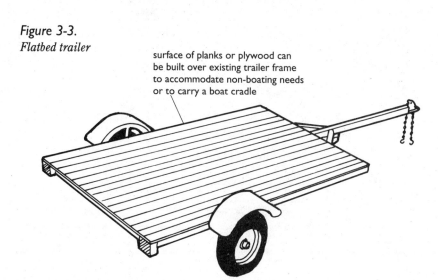

brackets on each side, bolted to the trailer frame for adjustability. Then you can substitute new wood 2 x 4s or 2 x 6s in the same slots that held the bunks, bolt them in place, and nail, screw, or bolt a planked or plywood deck on top. Use galvanized fasteners to extend the life of your flatbed. For hold-down attachment points, be sure to use eyebolts or other devices firmly attached to the trailer frame or the 2 x 4s bolted to it.

Conclusion: If first-cost economy is a top priority, you plan to use ramps only occasionally, and the ramps you use are reasonably steep, go for a bunk-type trailer. If you plan to launch and retrieve frequently, and you want to be able to launch on all kinds of ramps and minimize the hassles of launching and retrieving, try a roller type. But if your real interest is in clearing the brush out of the back forty or making twice-a-week runs to the town dump, and you only want to launch your deep-keel sailboat from her cradle once each spring and retrieve her once each fall, you might want to consider a flatbed trailer or a convertible bunk-to-flatbed unit.

Choosing the Right Size

Most boat trailers come in various sizes as measured by two main parameters, weight capacity and boat length. Trailer manufacturers usually list both these parameters in sales brochure specifications, but the manufacturer's identification plate on the trailer is not required to list maximum boat-length capacity and often doesn't. That's partly because government regulations classify recreational boat trailers according to weight capacity (as per Figure 3-4), not boat length, and partly because it's often difficult to pin down exact capacity in terms of boat length. In some instances a trailer specified in a catalog to support a given maximum weight and length of boat might be suitable for a boat of the same weight but several feet longer. By and large, however, it's best to rely on catalog data.

Figure 3-4.
Trailer and hitch classes and capacities

Trailer and Hitch Class	General Category	Maximum Capacity		Type of Hitch	Typical Tow-Vehicle Attachment Points
		Towing Weight t.w. (lbs.)	Tongue Weight (percent of t.w.)		
Class I	Light duty	2,000	10%	Fixed ball platform	Bumper plus two points on frame
Class II	Regular duty	3,500	10%	Fixed ball platform	Bumper plus two points on frame
Class III	Heavy duty	3,500 to 5,000	10%	Receiver type	Four or more points on frame
Class IV	Extra-heavy duty	5,000 to 10,000	10%	Receiver type	Four or more points on frame

"Trailer size" can also involve the width between fenders. In general, whether the fender-to-fender dimension is important to a particular buyer depends largely on whether his boat's hull chines will ride above or below the tops of the fenders. If the hull lies between the fenders (putting it lower to the ground and thus making ramp launching easier), the trailer may have to be somewhat wider than if the boat is raised above the fenders.

If you're thinking of a wide trailer, you should be aware that trailers with overall widths of 80 inches or more have considerably more complex lighting equipment compared with narrower vehicles. Extra width also entails longer axles and wider support beams, which add to first cost. On the other hand, wide trailers offer extra stability at highway speeds. Final choice of width in the long run is not necessarily clear-cut; it can involve balancing the pluses and minuses of your circumstances.

How to Figure the Trailer
Capacity You Need

To calculate the capacity you should aim for, start with the bare weight of your boat, available from the manufacturer and usually mentioned in sales literature. Add the weight of the motor and controls (sometimes included in the boat weight in sales literature, sometimes not). Then add the weight of accessories such as a canvas dodger, cushions, anchor and chain, lines, cabinetry, and other options not included in the base weight specification. Also add the weight of water, fuel, and oil you might carry aboard, assuming full tanks. (Fresh water weighs about 8.3 pounds per gallon; gasoline weighs 6.2 pounds per gallon; oil weighs about 7 pounds per gallon.) Finally figure the extras you'll store in the boat: portable ice chest stocked with beverages and food; groceries; spare parts; and so on.

With all these weights summed, you might want to add in a safety factor of perhaps 10% to arrive at your needed "trailer weight capacity." Look for a trailer with that capacity or a bit more; don't try to skimp or let your dealer talk you into an undersized or borderline trailer. On the other hand, don't get a lot more capacity than you need; the stiff ride of the heavier suspension could damage your hull.

To help you estimate the components of total weight for your boat and motor, Figure 3-5 shows typical bare boat weights (i.e. weight without fuel, accessories, gear, people, etc.), and Figure 3-6 indicates typical engine weights by horsepower.

Actual boat and engine weights vary widely depending on brand, so if you know your bare boat and engine weight or can get it from your dealer or the manufacturer, use it rather than the numbers from the tables.

While we're talking about weights, it might be well to mention the weight of the trailer itself. Most off-the-shelf steel recreational trailers weigh roughly as shown in Figure 3-7. Equivalent aluminum models may weigh 10 to 30% less.

Here again, weight can vary considerably depending on brand. If you know the trailer weight (which should be shown both on the tag on the trailer tongue and on the vehicle registration certificate), use it rather than the typical value. In any case, you'll need to know trailer weight before you can determine what tow

Figure 3-5.
Typical trailerable bare boat weights

Boat Length Overall (feet)	Bare Boat Weight in Pounds (see note)			
	Open Powerboats	Cruising Powerboats	Open Sailboats	Cruising Sailboats
10	250	—	80	—
11	250	—	100	—
12	300	—	130	—
13	400	—	170	—
14	500	1,500	230	800
15	700	2,000	300	1,000
16	1,000	2,600	400	1,200
17	1,600	2,800	550	1,400
18	2,000	3,000	900	1,600
19	2,300	3,200	1,050	1,800
20	2,400	3,500	1,200	2,000
21	2,800	4,000	1,600	2,400
22	3,200	4,500	1,800	2,800
23	3,600	5,000	2,000	3,200
24	4,000	5,500	2,200	3,800
25	4,500	6,000	2,400	4,600
26	5,000	6,500	2,700	5,400
27	5,500	7,000	3,000	6,200
28	—	7,500	3,300	7,000
29	—	8,500	3,600	8,000
30	—	10,000	4,000	9,000

Note: These boat weights, which include engine weight for "cruising" boats but not for "open" boats, are typical averages. Actual weights may vary by as much as plus-or-minus 40 percent or more.

vehicle to use (Chapters 5 and 6 plus Appendix 2), since the towing capacity of cars and trucks is rated against the sum of the weight of the boat, motor, and gear plus the weight of the trailer.

Matching Trailer to Boat Shape

Most trailers have multiple adjustment points, but not even the most adjustable trailer can be fitted successfully to every boat. You'll want a trailer with supports that properly match the shape of the boat for which it's intended (Figure 3-8). In judging whether a given trailer will fit your boat, there are several things to look for besides overall trailer length and width between the fenders. First, the supports should be placed at reinforced areas on the hull (such as at bulkheads and along lifting strakes and keel) to protect against damage to the hull. Second, there should be a sufficient number of support locations both under the hull and along the sides and bow to avoid excessive pressure at any one site, as well as to prevent side or forward movement when towing around bends in the road or during sudden stops. Third, the supports should be placed to carry the boat as low as possible, both for easier ramp launching and to keep the center of gravity of the load close to the road. (For this reason, drop axles and vee-shaped cross-members are often preferable to straight ones.) And fourth, the supports should be located so that when the boat is moving along the trailer during launching or loading at a ramp, the hull is continuously centered and doesn't scrape along unpadded parts of the trailer.

Figure 3-6.
Typical outboard engine weights

Engine Horsepower	Weight (lbs.)	Engine Horsepower	Weight (lbs.)
4	50	6	60
8	70	10	80
15	90	20	100
25	110	30	120
40	150	50	180
75	220	100	340
120	370	150	380
175	390	200	400
225	450	275	540
300	540		

Figure 3-7.
Typical trailer weights

Boat Length Overall (feet)	Trailer Weights in Pounds (see notes)			
	Single-axle Trailers		Tandem-axle Trailers	
	Light Duty	Heavy Duty	Light Duty	Heavy Duty
10 - 12	160 (400)	240 (600)	Use single-axle trailer	
11 - 13	160 (400)	240 (600)	"	"
12 - 14	160 (400)	240 (600)	"	"
13 - 15	180 (600)	300 (800)	"	"
14 - 16	200 (800)	350 (1,200)	"	"
15 - 17	400 (1,200)	500 (1,600)	425 (2,200)	450 (2,600)
16 - 18	500 (1,600)	575 (2,000)	550 (2,300)	650 (3,000)
17 - 19	550 (2,000)	600 (2,400)	650 (2,400)	850 (3,200)
18 - 20	600 (2,300)	700 (3,000)	700 (2,500)	1,050 (3,600)
19 - 21	800 (2,500)	950 (3,600)	850 (2,700)	1,200 (4,000)
20 - 22	900 (2,800)	1,150 (4,300)	950 (3,000)	1,300 (5,000)
21 - 23	950 (3,300)	1,350 (5,000)	1,050 (3,600)	1,400 (6,000)
22 - 24	1,000 (3,600)	1,500 (5,600)	1,080 (4,200)	1,500 (7,000)
23 - 25	1,200 (4,300)	1,600 (6,500)	1,250 (4,800)	1,700 (8,000)
24 - 26	1,400 (4,800)	1,700 (7,000)	1,500 (5,400)	2,000 (9,000)
25 - 27	1,600 (5,500)	2,000 (7,400)	1,700 (6,000)	2,300 (10,000)
26 - 28	Use tandem-axle trailer		1,800 (6,600)	2,600 (11,000)
27 - 29	"	"	2,000 (7,200)	3,000 (12,000)
28 - 30	"	"	2,200 (7,600)	3,600 (14,000)
29 - 31	"	"	2,400 (8,000)	4,200 (15,500)
30 - 32	"	"	2,700 (8,500)	4,800 (17,000)
31 - 35	"	"	3,000 (9,000)	5,200 (18,000)

Note: Trailer weight is in pounds, and adjacent number in parentheses is typical trailer capacity.
Sum of trailer weight plus capacity is maximum Gross Vehicle Weight Rating (GVWR). Data in table are approximate; actual weights vary considerably.

Figure 3-8.
Matching the trailer to boat shape

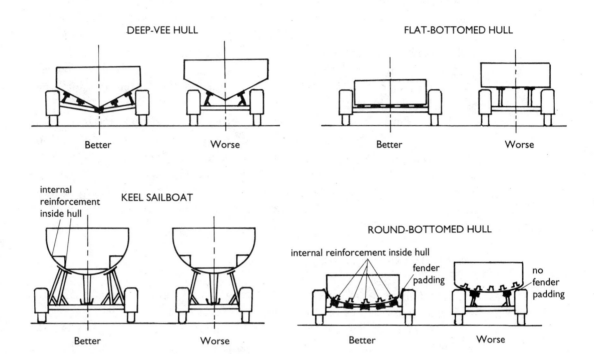

A trailer is well matched to the boat it carries if: (1) has supports that are placed well with regard to reinforcements in hull skin; (2) has many supports and a large support area, preventing heavy load concentration with consequent hull deflection; (3) has keel rollers or a bunk on the trailer centerline if the boat is strongest along the keel and has a relatively thin skin elsewhere; (4) has side supports relatively far apart, which helps to minimize the boat's tendency to sway on the trailer during transport; (5) has a relatively large track width (the distance between wheels on the same axle), which avoids forcing the hull weight higher and thus helps to keep the center of gravity as low as possible.

While there can never be too many supports for safety, the economics can begin to look unattractive as extra roller arms and padded brackets are installed — and so can the extra friction during a launch. In the final analysis, the best trailer designs usually call for just enough supports to hold the boat solidly in place without stress or strain while riding, and to guide it smoothly off and on while launching and retrieving in all conditions including crosswinds. Exception: If a trailer is designed for a sailboat supported at the keel plus two points on each side, a third support on each side can be very handy for coating the boat's bottom seasonally with antifouling paint.

To explain: Let's say your fin-keel sailboat is basically supported by her keel but held in place by six jackscrew-equipped shores, three on each side. To paint, first lower the center support on each side, and cover the whole bottom except under the four remaining shores. When that coat is dry, replace the two supports you dropped and let down two others — being careful never to lower any two that will allow the boat to tip. Repeat the process once more, and the job is finished.

Straight Axle or Drop Axle?

Figure 3-9 shows two styles of axles, "straight" and "drop." The so-called drop axle, usually lowered by approximately 4 inches, permits the keel of the boat to sit correspondingly lower inside the trailer frame, making it easier to launch in shallow water. Since the boat is lower, so is the center of gravity of the load, making for a generally smoother and more stable ride.

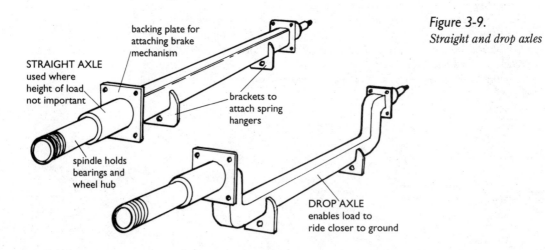

Figure 3-9.
Straight and drop axles

On the negative side, drop axles reduce road clearance, making it more diffi-cult to tow on rough or rutted roads. They are also more expensive to manufac-ture, and therefore the price of a trailer with drop axles is apt to be higher. In the final analysis, unless you're having a trailer custom built, your choice of straight or drop axles is likely to be based more than anything else on what's offered on the trailer brands accessible to you.

What About Suspension?

There are four ways a trailer frame may be suspended from its axles: leaf springs, coil springs, torsion bars, or with just a solid metal-to-metal connection.

A solid connection between frame and axle is not recommended for any roadworthy boat trailer, since the boat will get jounced around so much that damage to the hull is almost certain. Axles also break quite easily on trailers with no springs for the same reason. No commercial trailer makers sell such beasts as far as I know, but you might find a homemade one for sale. If you're serious about taking your boat on the road, don't buy it.

Figure 3-10 shows the three remaining types. *Leaf springs* are most common, and are used for all kinds of loads from a 140-pound Laser (needing a spring with but one leaf) to heavy boats requiring big springs with seven or more leaves. They come in two basic types: double-eye, or eye-and-slipper. Neither is inher-ently more effective than the other. Both permit easy access for inspection and maintenance.

Coil springs are sometimes used for relatively light loads, often in conjunc-tion with shock absorbers. They give a notably soft, cushioned ride and have no major drawbacks except for the comparative intricacy of their design. Perhaps their complexity is the reason they are becoming increasingly less common on boat trailers.

Torsion bars, designed to resist torsional, or twisting, motion, are new to the boat-trailer world within the last decade or so. They are totally self-contained, so there's no need for hangers, shackles, or other conventional suspension compo-nents. Due to their configuration, they can often be mounted to reduce frame height, thus lowering the center of gravity and making for a stabler ride. Another nice feature is that each wheel can have independent suspension, so one wheel can absorb a road shock without affecting any of the others. Installation is sim-ple, a matter of bolting brackets on the outer tube directly to the trailer frame. They're available in capacities from 2,000 to 6,000 pounds per axle. About the only objections to them are (1) that they cost more than conventional axles (though installation cost may be lower), and (2) that if water gets inside the outer tube of a nongalvanized unit, unseen corrosion may develop.

Figure 3-10.
Types of suspension

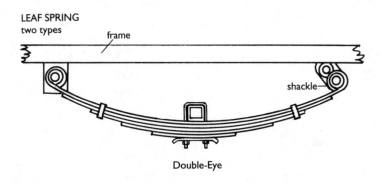

LEAF SPRING
two types

Double-Eye

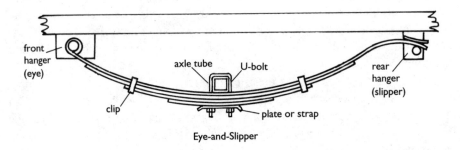

Eye-and-Slipper

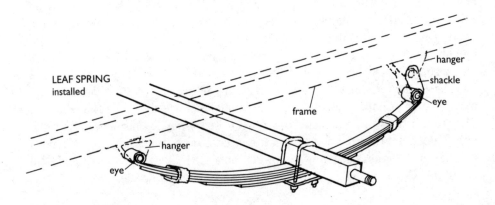

LEAF SPRING
installed

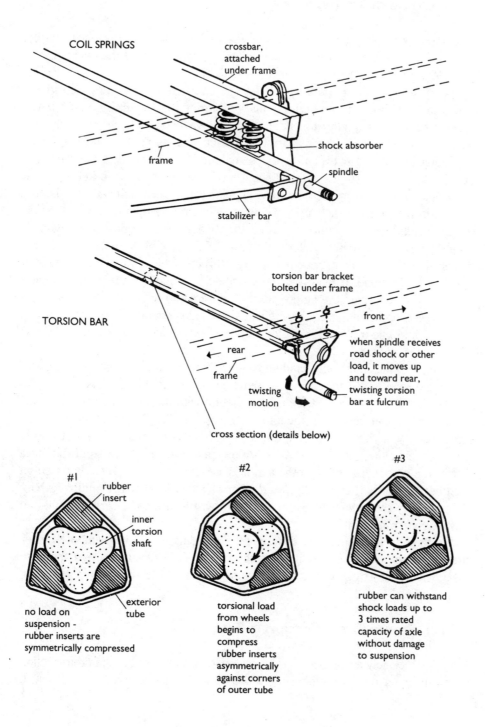

COIL SPRINGS

crossbar,
attached
under frame

shock absorber

spindle

frame

stabilizer bar

TORSION BAR

torsion bar bracket
bolted under frame

front →

← rear

frame

twisting
motion

when spindle receives
road shock or other
load, it moves up
and toward rear,
twisting torsion
bar at fulcrum

cross section (details below)

#1

rubber
insert

inner
torsion
shaft

exterior
tube

no load on
suspension -
rubber inserts are
symmetrically compressed

#2

torsional load
from wheels
begins to
compress
rubber inserts
asymmetrically
against corners
of outer tube

#3

rubber can withstand
shock loads up to
3 times rated
capacity of axle
without damage
to suspension

Single Axle or Tandem?

A tandem-axle trailer, such as shown in Figure 3-2, has two or three axles rather than just one. A tandem trailer generally can carry more load than a single-axle vehicle of the same frame size, since the weight of the load is spread over more tires, springs, support points, and so on. Tandem-axle trailers also give a smoother ride both on the highway and on bumpy rural roads, and offer better tracking and less tendency to fishtail than single-axle types. Tongue weight isn't as sensitive to the load shifting forward or back, as long as the center of gravity of the load is located between the axles, making it less likely that a load-equalizing hitch, helper springs, or other such device will be needed to keep the tow vehicle's back end from sagging. And smaller wheels can be used because the weight is distributed over four road contact points rather than two, which in turn permits reducing the frame height by the difference in radius of the wheels, thereby further improving trailer stability. In addition, a blowout on the highway is less likely to have disastrous results with three wheels left to support the load rather than just one. It may even be possible, by removing the blown tire and wheel and cinching up the empty hub to the frame, to travel on three wheels to the nearest repair station. In this respect, three axles are even better than two — though triple-axle trailers, except for extremely large, heavy boats pulled by full-sized trucks, are rare.

On the other hand, with tandem trailers there are more tires, bearings, suspension elements, etc. to service. Maneuverability is slightly impaired because of the tendency to track in a straight line (though with no load on a twin-axle trailer, you can sometimes lower the tongue enough to raise the back wheels off the ground, so you can maneuver the trailer by hand around a parking lot on the front wheels alone). Tandems are more expensive to buy because of the extra parts, and cost more at tollbooths and in state taxes when payment is based on number of axles. Incidentally, tandem trailers without load-equalizing bars (Figure 3-11) can behave badly on the highway. Be sure equalizers are built into any tandem trailer you buy.

In the final analysis, many boat people (including me) believe that whenever the size of the load warrants it (starting at about 2,600 pounds or so) the positives of tandem axles far outweigh the negatives — including their generally higher price .

Which Frame Cross Section is Best?

If you look closely at the frame of a boat trailer, you'll see that the cross-section shape of its structural members is probably a "C" (a "channel"), an "I" (an I-beam), an "O" (a round tube), or a box (a square or rectangular tube), as illustrated in Figure 3-12. Each section has its own strength characteristics. For a given height, width, and metal thickness, a rectangular or square tube is strongest overall, and a round tube is a close second, since both are stronger in torsion than a similarly sized "C" or "I" section. But closed tubes have a drawback when used in water: Their inside walls tend to rust. If the tubes are galvanized inside and out this problem virtually disappears, but painted tubes — unless they're dipped into a paint vat, a practice used by only a few manufacturers — definitely have a shorter life expectancy than painted "C" or "I" sections.

A deep section is stronger than a shallow section of the same metal thickness in bending (often the main type of force acting on a trailer), so between two

Figure 3-11.
Load-equalizing bar

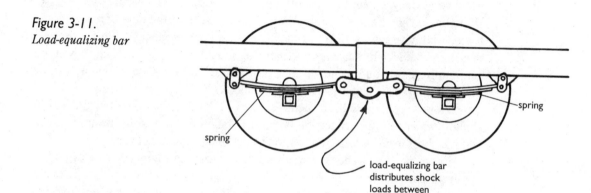

spring

spring

load-equalizing bar
distributes shock
loads between
adjoining springs

Figure 3-12.
Frame cross sections

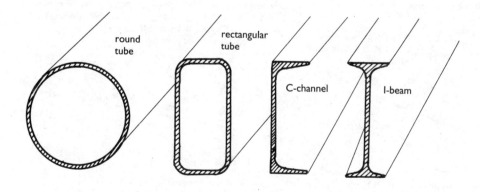

round
tube

rectangular
tube

C-channel

I-beam

trailers rated for the same load, the deeper section (if otherwise similar in shape) will generally be more durable. And of course, a thick section will be more durable than a thin one of the same size and shape, not only because of greater stiffness, but also because if rust eats away the surface, more solid metal will be left in the thicker section.

Do You Need a Tilt Bed?

A tilt-bed trailer (Figure 3-13) has a hinged tongue that can be unlatched, supposedly for easier launching and retrieving at low-slope launching ramps. But while raising the front end of the bed like a dump truck and letting the boat simply slide downhill into the water may sound good, in real life it often doesn't work very easily except for boats that weigh less than a thousand pounds or so. If the boat is any heavier, the bed, which pivots around the axle of a single-axle trailer, will not be easy to tilt up — unless the boat is balanced almost directly over the axle, which is farther aft than she should be for proper tongue weight. And by the time you get her to that position, she'll be rolling aft anyway. (For more on this, see Chapter 9 on handling basics.)

Another problem with tilt beds is that when a deep-vee boat is launched in shallow water, there may not be enough flotation in the vee of the transom to keep the boat from sliding right off the trailer and onto the bottom.

Moreover, if the trailer has double axles, on most designs you can forget tilting even if the tongue is hinged. To lift the front end of the bed will be virtually impossible until the boat's weight is centered aft of the back axle; even then you have to actually lift the front tires off the ground to tilt the bed. And by that time the boat's transom will probably be afloat, eliminating the need.

In summary: Unless your boat is relatively light and easy to shove around on the trailer, it often won't pay to try using the tilt function, even if it's available.

Figure 3-13.

Tilt-bed trailer in "tilt" position

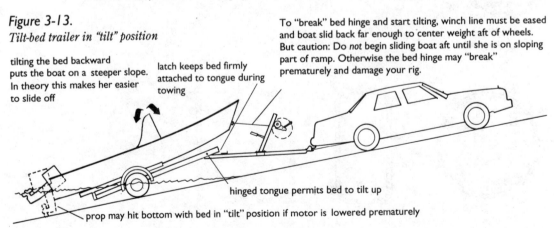

tilting the bed backward puts the boat on a steeper slope. In theory this makes her easier to slide off

latch keeps bed firmly attached to tongue during towing

To "break" bed hinge and start tilting, winch line must be eased and boat slid back far enough to center weight aft of wheels. But caution: Do *not* begin sliding boat aft until she is on sloping part of ramp. Otherwise the bed hinge may "break" prematurely and damage your rig.

hinged tongue permits bed to tilt up

prop may hit bottom with bed in "tilt" position if motor is lowered prematurely

A-Frame or Pole Tongue?

Figure 3-14 shows a bird's-eye view of A-frame and pole-tongue models, the two predominant designs in use today. Heavy-duty trailers usually have A-frames, which more easily accept weight-distributing hitches (sometimes called "load-equalizing hitches"; see Chapter 7 for a detailed description). Pole-tongue models, many of which have the tilt-frame feature, are typically used to carry lighter loads, but may also be used for heavy loads and can even accommodate some brands of weight-distributing hitches if a pole-tongue adapter is used. Still, which type of frame you choose depends mainly on how big a load you plan to carry, with A-frames definitely more popular — and usually more costly — in the larger sizes.

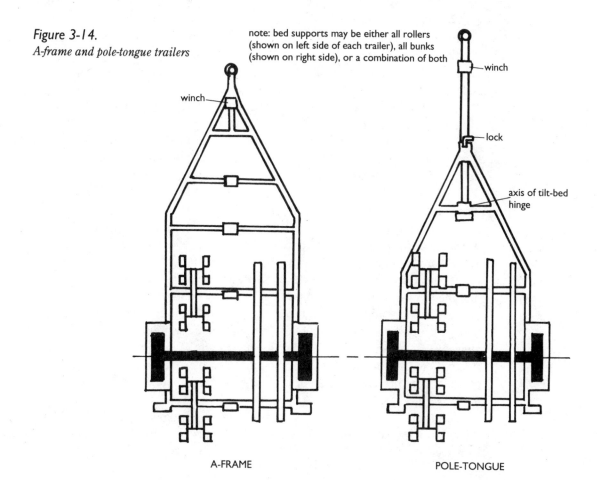

Figure 3-14.
A-frame and pole-tongue trailers

note: bed supports may be either all rollers (shown on left side of each trailer), all bunks (shown on right side), or a combination of both

A-FRAME

POLE-TONGUE

Checking Out Required Labeling and Equipment

Both federal and state governments have rules for boat trailers; so does the boating industry's group, the National Marine Manufacturers Association (NMMA). A rundown on the principal state-by-state recreational trailer regulations is presented in Appendix 1. Important details on labeling and equipment are as follows.

Trailer Labeling Requirements

According to NMMA rules, a label must be placed on the front half of the left side of the trailer, either on the tongue or the main frame. It should state the name of the manufacturer, month and year that manufacture was completed, the Gross Vehicle Weight Rating (GVWR) in pounds, the Gross Axle Weight Rating (GAWR) in pounds in sequence from front to rear, the tire size including load range, and the Vehicle Identification Number. Before buying a trailer, always check the label information against the vehicle registration data supplied by the seller to be sure it matches. If it doesn't and you buy anyway, you could be the receiver of stolen goods.

The *GVWR* is the loaded weight of the trailer, i.e. the sum of the rated carrying capacity of the trailer plus the weight of the trailer itself.

The *GAWR* is the load-carrying capacity of an axle. For multi-axle trailers, the sum of the combined GAWRs equals the GVWR; by law, no credit is allowed for whatever weight may be supported by the trailer hitch.

Tire Size

A tire's capacity must not be less than its share of the gross axle rating. In other words, if a GAWR is 3,500 pounds, each tire on that axle must be rated to at least 1,750 pounds of capacity. When buying a trailer, new or used, or when buying replacement tires, always check to be sure each tire's capacity is at least equal to half the GAWR, and know that capacity can vary considerably among tires of a single size, depending on tire construction as defined by "load range." I once bought a trailer on which somebody, probably unknowingly, had substituted relatively weak load-range "B" tires for the load-range "C" tires required by the axle rating. I didn't notice the discrepancy until a tire blew out on I-95. Data showing typical trailer tire sizes, inflation pressures, capacities, and load ranges appear in Figure 10-1.

Naturally, the higher load ranges are the most expensive. When you see trailer tires on sale, they're almost always the lower load ranges — so check before you buy.

Lights and Safety Reflectors

Figures 3-15 and 3-16 indicate trailer lighting requirements for trailers less than 80 inches and for those 80 or more inches wide, respectively. The wider trailers require significantly more complicated lighting, and if the trailer is 30 feet long or longer, even more stringent requirements apply. It's also worth noting that some states have mins and maxes on taillight height above the road, typically 15 inches (minimum) to 72 inches (maximum).

Trailer Coupler and Ball Classes

We'll cover hitches and hitch balls more thoroughly later in the book, but this is a good place to mention the legal requirements for couplers and balls. As you may already know, a trailer tongue is connected to its tow vehicle by a coupler, in the form of a socket that fits snugly around a mating steel ball bolted to the tow-vehicle trailer hitch. What you may *not* know is that the government has strict requirements for both coupler and ball, and that not all 1⅞-inch or 2-inch diameter balls or couplers are the same. Capacities are stamped on both ball and coupler. The ratings are as shown in Figure 3-17.

Figure 3-15.
Lights for trailers less than 80 inches wide

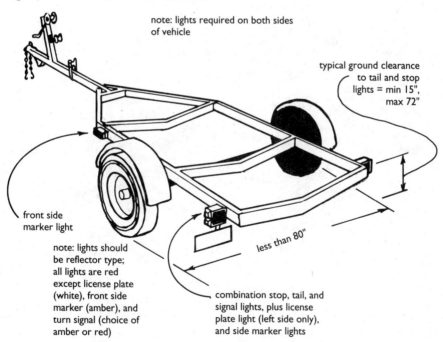

note: lights required on both sides of vehicle

typical ground clearance to tail and stop lights = min 15", max 72"

front side marker light

note: lights should be reflector type; all lights are red except license plate (white), front side marker (amber), and turn signal (choice of amber or red)

less than 80"

combination stop, tail, and signal lights, plus license plate light (left side only), and side marker lights

Safety Chains

The NMMA specs call for a safety chain strong enough to withstand a 2,000-pound minimum breaking load for Class I trailers, 3,500 pounds for Class II, and 5,000 pounds for Class III. Strength must be equal to the trailer's gross weight for Class IV. In terms of strength of specific sizes of proof coil chain, this translates to the numbers in Figure 3-18.

Brakes

Requirements for trailer brakes vary by state, and some tow-vehicle manufacturers require trailer brakes above certain load limits. See Appendixes 1 and 2 for details. In addition, the NMMA standards call for their member manufacturers to offer brakes for all wheels of trailers with a 1,500-pound GVWR or more. But "offered" does not mean "installed," so if you want trailer brakes, whether for one axle or all axles, don't assume the trailer you're buying has them just because it's a big one.

Figure 3-16.
Lights for trailers 80 inches or more in width

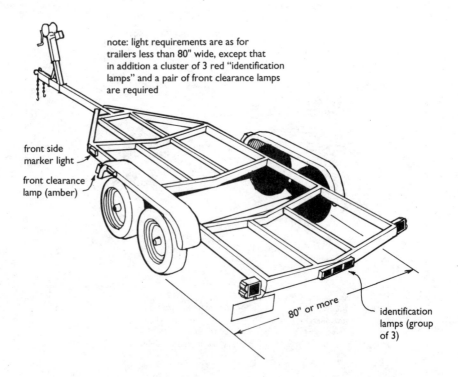

note: light requirements are as for trailers less than 80" wide, except that in addition a cluster of 3 red "identification lamps" and a pair of front clearance lamps are required

front side marker light

front clearance lamp (amber)

80" or more

identification lamps (group of 3)

Figure 3-17.
Strength ratings for trailer couplers and balls

Trailer Classification	Class I	Class II	Class III	Class IV
Maximum GVWR (lbs.)	2,000	3,500	5,000	10,000
Coupler Designation	No. 1	No. 2	No. 3	No. 4
Minimum ball diameter (inches)	1 7/8	2	2	2 5/16
Minimum breaking-point requirements:				
Longitudinal tension and compression (lbs.)	6,000	10,500	15,000	3 times the gross trailer weight
Transverse thrust (lbs.)	2,000	3,000	4,000	Equal to gross trailer weight
Vertical tension and compression (lbs.)	2,500	4,500	7,000	1.3 times gross trailer weight

Figure 3-18.
Safety chain strength required for various trailer classes

Proof-Coil Chain Size (link thickness) (inches)	Breaking Strength (lbs.)	For Trailer Class
1/8	Not acceptable	—
3/16	3,000	Class I
1/4	5,000	Classes II and III
5/16	7,600	Class IV *
3/8	10,600	Class IV *
7/16	14,000	Class IV *

* Chain can be used with trailer size shown provided gross trailer weight does not exceed breaking strength shown. Double chains are required.

Boat trailer brakes must be of a type that operate automatically when the towing vehicle's service brakes are applied or when, while being pulled, the trailer becomes separated from the tow vehicle. There are two types of trailer brakes that fit this description: (1) surge brakes, controlled by an actuator mounted at the forward end of the trailer, and (2) trailer brakes physically linked to the tow-vehicle brake system. The latter are usually electrically operated, while the former are usually hydraulically actuated. Since boat trailers are almost always designed to be occasionally submerged, and since water and electricity don't mix well, you should opt for surge brakes and avoid electric brakes unless you *never* expect to submerge your wheels.

One more caveat: Some surge brake systems won't operate properly when a weight-distribution hitch or sway-control device is in use. See Chapter 7 for additional information on this subject.

Deciding on Paint, Galvanizing, or Other Finish

Although a few trailers (such as those made by Trailex, Boat Master, and Crown) are constructed of anodized or polished aluminum, most boat trailers today are either galvanized or painted steel.

Galvanized steel is clearly a better choice than paint for salt water if the trailer will be dunked frequently, provided the buyer's budget will permit the several hundred dollars extra cost for galvanizing. But a painted finish may stand up for many years even when used in salt water, if regular care is taken to recoat any bare spots with rust-preventative paint such as Rustoleum's Derusto Rust Preventive Primer #883/MP-100 or Pettit's Trailercoat #6981.

Even with Derusto or Trailercoat, though, rust will slowly but inevitably keep surfacing, and eventually weakened frame members will have to be replaced. This may not happen as fast as you think; I just finished replacing the main frame and tongue on one of my trailers, a 20-year-old veteran used exclusively (but sparingly) in salt water. The rest of the trailer (axles, fenders, crossbeams, etc.) is still all original, and going strong.

Aluminum is even more costly than galvanized steel, but to some folks may be worth the premium. The neat appearance of shiny aluminum adds to the value of the low-maintenance finish; an occasional freshwater rinse is all you need to keep the surface looking new. But be prepared to spend a premium of 20 to 100% compared with an equivalent painted trailer.

A Word About Specialty Trailers

Sometimes boat people need special trailers for special purposes. Luckily, there's no end to the ingenuity of some custom trailer builders, and if you need a special trailer, you can almost certainly get it. Figures 3-19, 3-20, and 3-21 show a few of the clever ideas I've come across. Where the manufacturer's name is given, you'll find the address in Appendix 3.

The vast array of trailer accessories are worth a whole chapter by themselves — as you'll see on the next page.

Figure 3-19.
Keel Hauler

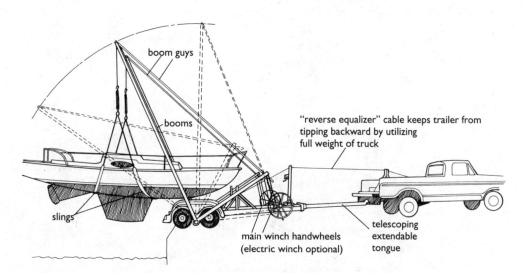

The Keel Hauler offered by Brooks Sales and Engineering is a self-loading trailer for fixed-keel sailboats up to 30 feet long and weighing up to 5,000 pounds. The triangular lifting rig removes and stows for transport. Using the main winch handwheels, one or two people can lift 2 tons with a combined force of only 60 pounds.

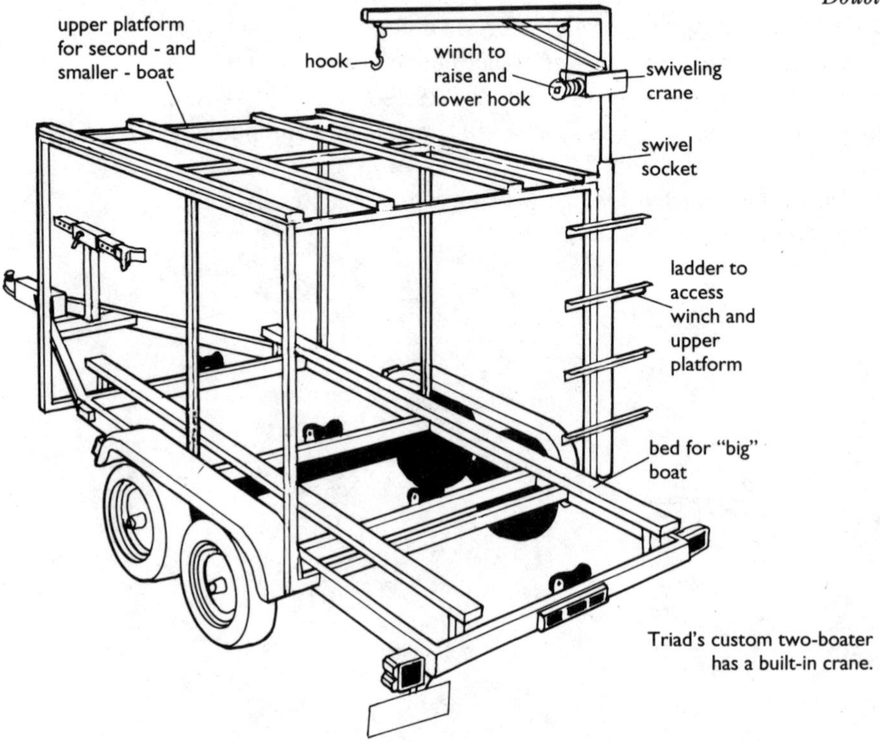

Figure 3-20.
Double-decker trailer

upper platform
for second - and
smaller - boat

hook

winch to
raise and
lower hook

swiveling
crane

swivel
socket

ladder to
access
winch and
upper
platform

bed for "big"
boat

Triad's custom two-boater
has a built-in crane.

Figure 3-21.

*Trailer for a small sailboat
(130-pound Laser racing
boat)*

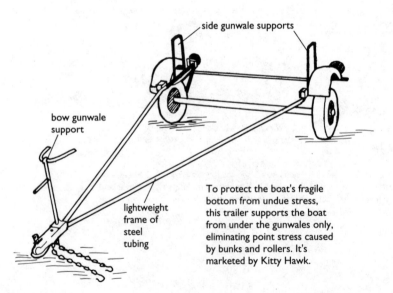

side gunwale supports

bow gunwale
support

lightweight
frame of
steel
tubing

To protect the boat's fragile
bottom from undue stress,
this trailer supports the boat
from under the gunwales only,
eliminating point stress caused
by bunks and rollers. It's
marketed by Kitty Hawk.

CHAPTER FOUR

Picking Trailer Accessories

Not every trailer needs a tongue jack, walkway, guide bars, or other optional paraphernalia. In fact, add-on accessories can sometimes be more hindrance than help. Here's a rundown on the variety of trailer accessories available, with some comments on their advantages and disadvantages.

Winches

A winch (Figure 4-1) is used to control movement of a boat as it is launched and retrieved at a ramp, and to help prevent boat movement during road travel. Winches are found on practically every small powerboat trailer (even though some vendors sell them as an optional extra). They are available in three basic types: one-speed manual, two-speed manual, and electric-power operated. Each type has its pluses and minuses.

One-speed manual winches are designed to handle small boats weighing up to 2,000 to 2,500 pounds. But not all one-speed winches are the same; some have a lot more pulling power than others. Winch manufacturers offer a wide range of combinations of gear ratios, handle lengths, and drum diameters, all of which — along with friction in the system and the structural strength rating (as stamped on the winch body) — affect a given winch's speed, power, or both.

As of this writing, suppliers' catalogs don't specify pulling power; you have to figure it out yourself, using the method described below or by referring to Figure 4-2, which gives pulling power for some common winch sizes. With a one-speed winch, you get either pulling power or speed; if you want to choose first one, then the other as the need demands, you'll need a two-speed winch.

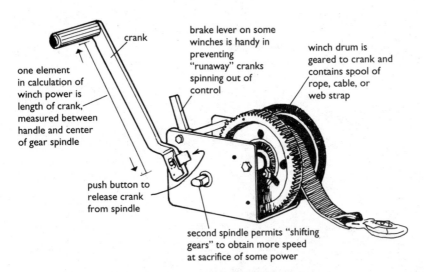

crank

brake lever on some
winches is handy in
preventing
"runaway" cranks
spinning out of
control

winch drum is
geared to crank and
contains spool of
rope, cable, or
web strap

one element
in calculation of
winch power is
length of crank,
measured between
handle and center
of gear spindle

push button to
release crank
from spindle

second spindle permits "shifting
gears" to obtain more speed
at sacrifice of some power

Figure 4-1.
Winch

To check pulling power, first calculate the winch's so-called power ratio
(PR). This is basically the overall theoretical mechanical advantage (disregard-
ing friction) of gear train, crank handle, and effective drum size. It is the number
of inches of movement at the input side of the winch (i.e. at the crank handle)
divided by the corresponding inches of movement at the output side (i.e. the
amount of line, cable, or heavy-duty nylon web strap pulled off the winch). In formula form:

$$PR = \frac{\text{crank length x gear ratio}}{\text{1/2 x effective drum diameter}}$$

The crank length is measured from the center of the axis at the handle end
of the crank to the center of the axis at the spindle end.

The gear ratio is determined simply by counting teeth. That is, if the small
gear on the crank spindle has 12 teeth and the driven gear on the drum has 36
teeth, the gear ratio is 3:1.

The *effective* drum diameter is not necessarily the diameter of the spool on
the drum. For example, if large-sized rope is used, the effective drum diameter
will gradually increase as layer upon layer of rope is wound up on the drum.
Thus, for instance, a 1-inch drum diameter with a 2-inch layer of line wound on it
will have an effective diameter of 5 inches.

To illustrate, suppose a certain winch has a crank 12 inches long, a gear ratio
of 3:1, and an effective drum diameter of 6 inches. Then:

$$PR = \frac{12 \text{ x } 3}{\text{1/2 x 6}} = 12.$$

Figure 4-2.
Pulling power of typical winches

Catalog Winch Capacity (lbs.)	Number of Speeds	Gear Ratio (xx:1)	Crank Length (Inches)	Pulling Power (lbs.)
600	1	3.1	6	372
800	1	3.2	6	384
1,000	1	4.1	7	574
1,200	1	4.1	8	656
1,400	1	4.1	9	738
1,700	2	5.5 + 10.5	9	990 + 1,890
1,800	1	5.1	9	918
2,000	2	5.5 + 12.5	9	990 + 2,250
2,200	2	4.1 + 9.8	10	820 + 1,960
2,500	2	5.1 + 12.2	10	1,020 + 2,440
2,500	2	5.5 + 17.0	10	1,100 + 3,400
2,600	2	5.1 + 12.2	10	1,020 + 2,440
3,500	2	6.0 + 12.0	12	1,440 + 2,880

Note: To calculate pulling power, friction is assumed to be 25%, drum diameter after line is wrapped is assumed to be 3", and pull on handle is assumed at 40 pounds.

But the PR is a theoretical value, ignoring friction. To get pulling power, you must take into account the resistance of the winch bearings and the winch line binding against itself. This may reduce actual pulling power by 25 or 30% — more if you haven't lubricated your winch lately. Assuming in the above example that the friction factor is 25% and you are capable of pulling on the handle with a force of 40 pounds, the overall system will have a pulling power of 12 x 75% x 40 = 360 pounds.

Two-speed manual winches are similar to one-speed types but have a high-speed gear for fast cranking and a low-speed gear for winching in that last few feet of line. The last little bit is often hardest to crank for several reasons: the full weight of the boat is being pulled, since none of it is left in the water; the boat is usually at its steepest attitude; friction against rollers and bunks is greatest when none of the load is supported by water; and the effective diameter of the winch drum is largest since most of its line is wound up on it. For these reasons, for boats weighing around 2,000 pounds or more, a low gear can be quite useful.

On most winches, gears are shifted simply by moving the crank from one spindle to another. That means a special, easily removable crank such as shown in Figure 4-1 is needed for two-speed winches. If you use a removable handle, you'll have to remember to stow it in the tow vehicle when not in use to guard against theft or loss en route by being jiggled off its spindle.

Electric power winches are the ultimate for no-effort retrieval of heavy boats on steep ramps. They are connected to the tow vehicle's battery by a wiring harness usually supplied by the maker, and can draw considerable current. Typically they draw 12 to 15 amps with no load, and up to 80 amps or more at full load; at 12 volts and 80 amps, that's almost 1,000 watts. Hence electric power winches require heavy-duty wiring, a circuit breaker for safety, and a high-capacity switch — which, incidentally, usually can be remotely operated.

Compared with manual winches, electrics demand a bit more coddling to keep them in top condition, and they are expensive. A typical price in 1990 for a 1,500-pound–capacity electric is $140, compared with only $66 for a typical 2,600-pound–capacity two-speed manual winch. If your power requirements are modest, you can buy a small single-speed manual model for as little as $16.

Winch Lines, Cables, and Straps

The connection between the winch and the boat's bow eye is generally either synthetic rope, galvanized or stainless steel cable, or woven synthetic (such as nylon) web strap. If a wide but thin nylon strap is substituted for the thick rope on the winch used to illustrate the "PR" discussion above, the effective drum diameter might be reduced from 6 inches to, say, 4 inches (but not to 1 inch; even the web strap has some thickness). The friction contributed by the rope binding on itself would also be eliminated, reducing frictional losses from 25% to, say, 20%. The combination of increased leverage and reduced friction would increase pulling power in the example from 360 pounds to 18 x 80% x 40 = 576 pounds, a significant improvement. There is some indication that nylon web strapping is less likely to snap than rope or cable, and it won't rust or break down as galvanized cable eventually will after an extended period of hard use. Furthermore, web strapping is fairly economical (around $10 to $12 for a 20-foot length with a forged steel hook already attached). All things considered, this relatively new alternative to rope or cable could be your best choice for pulling most boats onto most trailers.

Dollies and Jacks

Dollies and jacks come in a variety of types. *Tongue dollies* can be either manual or motorized, portable or permanently mounted on the trailer tongue. For yacht clubs or marinas catering to small trailerable boats, a *portable manual tongue dolly* (Figure 4-3) can be handy when moving trailers lacking their own permanently mounted dollies. But it might be hard to pull bigger boats (1,000 pounds plus) with a manual dolly, which is where *portable motorized tongue dollies* come in. (The only one I've seen of this kind, at a marina in Santa Cruz, California, appeared to be homemade from power lawnmower parts.)

Figure 4-3.
Portable tongue dolly

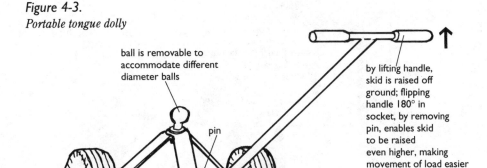

ball is removable to accommodate different diameter balls

pin

socket

skid

by lifting handle, skid is raised off ground; flipping handle 180° in socket, by removing pin, enables skid to be raised even higher, making movement of load easier

Individual permanently mounted tongue jacks — and permanently mounted dollies — are available, but a *combination tongue jack and dolly* (Figure 4-4) is usually preferable since it's more compact and easier to use. Moreover, a permanently mounted unit is better than a portable tongue dolly since it's always ready for instant use and can raise the tongue for coupling or uncoupling from the tow vehicle as well as make it easy to move a boat around a parking lot or yard.

A *stationary jack* — basically a combination jack/dolly with the dolly replaced by a welded steel foot — serves to lift the trailer and its load and to hold the trailer in place. When placed near the rear of the trailer, such a jack can keep the trailer from tipping backward when you wander aft on the loaded boat above, and helps prevent rolling when the trailer is sitting on a slight grade. (If the grade is steep enough, the jack foot will simply slide along the ground as the trailer moves; then a pair of wheel chocks will be needed.) But an upended 2 x 4 or concrete block wedged under the back end and held in place by raising the tongue jack (thus lowering the trailer's back end) can also help insure against tipping or rolling, negating much of the reason for investing in a stationary jack.

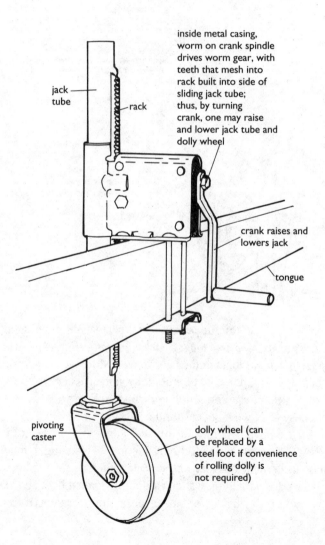

inside metal casing, worm on crank spindle drives worm gear, with teeth that mesh into rack built into side of sliding jack tube; thus, by turning crank, one may raise and lower jack tube and dolly wheel

jack tube

rack

crank raises and lowers jack

tongue

pivoting caster

dolly wheel (can be replaced by a steel foot if convenience of rolling dolly is not required)

Figure 4-4.
Combination tongue jack and dolly

Special Trailer Tongues

A *removable tongue* (Figure 4-5) is a good idea if you want to fit your boat and trailer into an ordinary garage but are prevented from doing so by the protruding pole tongue. Most pole tongues used on tilt-bed trailers are bolted in place, and are therefore removable by simply backing out the bolt at the pivot point. For off-season storage at a remote location such as a summer cottage, you can take the removed tongue home with you and leave the boat on its tongueless trailer to help prevent theft.

An *extension tongue* (Figure 4-6) works well where ramps are shallow or where the boat being launched has a deep underbody and therefore sits high on the trailer, requiring unusually deep water to float free. The extension tongue — either a separate structural member or the regular trailer tongue fitted so that it can telescope from a retracted to an extended position — enables the trailer to be backed far past the water's edge without submerging the back end of the tow vehicle.

Figure 4-5.
Removable tongue

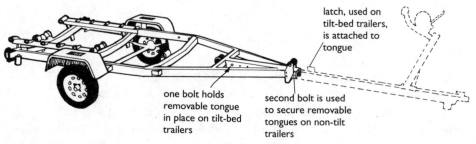

latch, used on tilt-bed trailers, is attached to tongue

one bolt holds removable tongue in place on tilt-bed trailers

second bolt is used to secure removable tongues on non-tilt trailers

Figure 4-6.
Extension tongue

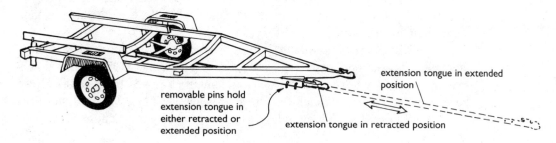

removable pins hold extension tongue in either retracted or extended position

extension tongue in extended position

extension tongue in retracted position

Spare Wheels and Brackets

A spare wheel mounted on a bracket welded or bolted to the trailer frame is an item many trailer boaters don't think about until they have their first flat on the highway. A trailer spare is highly recommended for anyone who wouldn't think of driving his *car* without a spare. Incidentally, some authorities suggest fitting the trailer with the same size wheel and tire as the tow vehicle so the same spare can be used for both. This generally is not a good idea; see Chapter 10 for the reasons.

Two types of carrying brackets are shown in Figure 4-7. The simple and popular design on the left features a U-bolt with ends spaced to fit the lug holes in most small trailer tires, and two arms that can be padlocked together to thwart wheel-stealers. It sells for a mere $4 to $5 and is available from a number of suppliers. In all the pictures I've seen of these devices, they are inexplicably shown upside down. The item is shown in the correct position here, with wheel over, not under the trailer tongue (which could give road-clearance problems), and lock on top (helping to keep road dirt out of the lock mechanism and making it easier to fit the key in the lock).

A "revolving spare tire carrier" marketed by Dutton-Lainson is pictured on the right. This device lets the spare tire serve as a dolly wheel when the trailer is disconnected from the tow vehicle. However, although the wheel revolves, it doesn't swivel, which makes steering the trailer through turns difficult when pushing by hand.

Automatic Coupling Devices

Two designs for automatic couplers are shown in Figures 4-8 and 4-9. Both are intended for folks who hitch up singlehandedly and are tired of having to back up four or five times to align the trailer ball directly under the coupler by trial and error. If you can back up within six inches of either side of the ball, and have a means of lifting the coupler to a precise height (such as with a jack/dolly) these devices will automatically center the hitch ball on the coupler. With the Hitch-Align unit (Figure 4-8), the driver lowers the coupler onto the ball. With the Auto-Hitch (Figure 4-9), the unit automatically lifts the trailer coupler up and drops it on the ball for you.

The Hitch-Align sells (in 1990) for $39.95. The Auto-Hitch, which is more automatic, is also more expensive; suggested retail price is $195. Another potential drawback is that it requires a 5-inch minimum clearance between the center of the ball and the tow vehicle's bumper to allow clearance for the Auto-Hitch mechanism. The Hitch-Align requires a clearance of only $2\frac{5}{8}$ inches.

Figure 4-7.
Two examples of spare-tire carrying brackets

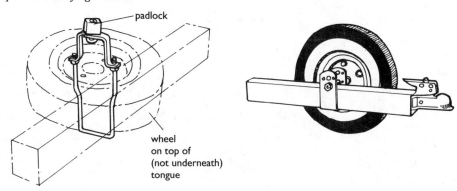

padlock

wheel
on top of
(not underneath)
tongue

Figure 4-8.
Hitch-Align unit

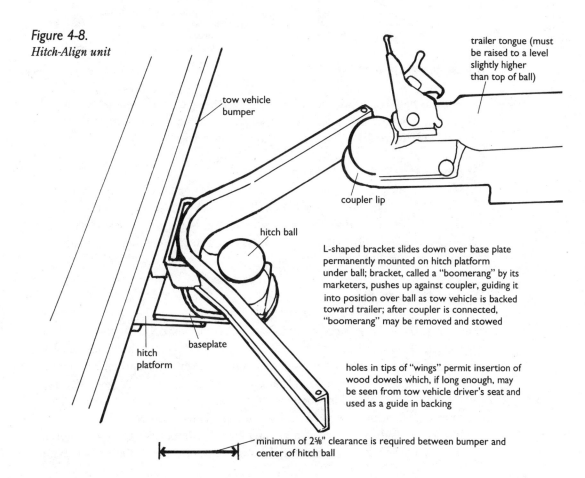

trailer tongue (must
be raised to a level
slightly higher
than top of ball)

tow vehicle
bumper

coupler lip

hitch ball

L-shaped bracket slides down over base plate
permanently mounted on hitch platform
under ball; bracket, called a "boomerang" by its
marketers, pushes up against coupler, guiding it
into position over ball as tow vehicle is backed
toward trailer; after coupler is connected,
"boomerang" may be removed and stowed

baseplate

hitch
platform

holes in tips of "wings" permit insertion of
wood dowels which, if long enough, may
be seen from tow vehicle driver's seat and
used as a guide in backing

minimum of 2⅝" clearance is required between bumper and
center of hitch ball

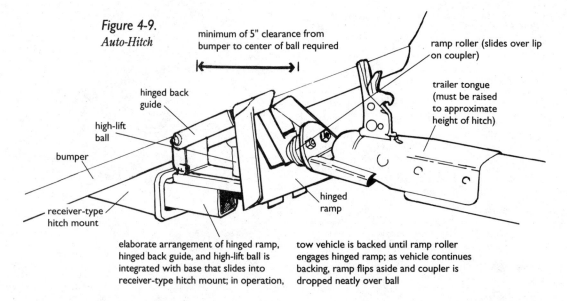

Figure 4-9.
Auto-Hitch

minimum of 5" clearance from
bumper to center of ball required

ramp roller (slides over lip
on coupler)

trailer tongue
(must be raised
to approximate
height of hitch)

hinged back
guide

high-lift
ball

bumper

hinged
ramp

receiver-type
hitch mount

elaborate arrangement of hinged ramp,
hinged back guide, and high-lift ball is
integrated with base that slides into
receiver-type hitch mount; in operation,

tow vehicle is backed until ramp roller
engages hinged ramp; as vehicle continues
backing, ramp flips aside and coupler is
dropped neatly over ball

Mast-Raising Gear

Devices to help trailer-sailors raise and lower hinged masts differ from boat to boat. Here just one installation — the scheme I use on my cruising catboat — is sketched in Figure 4-10. Variations on the theme are endless.

Storage Boxes

On-trailer storage can sometimes be built in if space can be found into which the boat hull doesn't encroach — and if submersion is not a problem. Figure 4-11 shows an example of built-in storage, typically used for one-design sailboats meant to be launched by a boat hoist.

Steps and Ladders

Steps to assist in boarding your boat can be helpful, especially when the deck is well above the road. You can often board a low-slung powerboat or daysailer just by stepping up on a fender and swinging your leg over the gunwale. If you intend to board this way, you can skidproof your fenders by applying paint sprinkled with sand or crushed walnut shells or by sticking on strips of 3M's nonskid tape.

For higher boats, a four- to six-foot portable ladder can be carried in the tow vehicle — or a ladder can be permanently built into the trailer any place there's a stout support such as a winch stand, bow support, or other vertical strut (Figure 3-21).

Figure 4-10.
Mast-raising gear

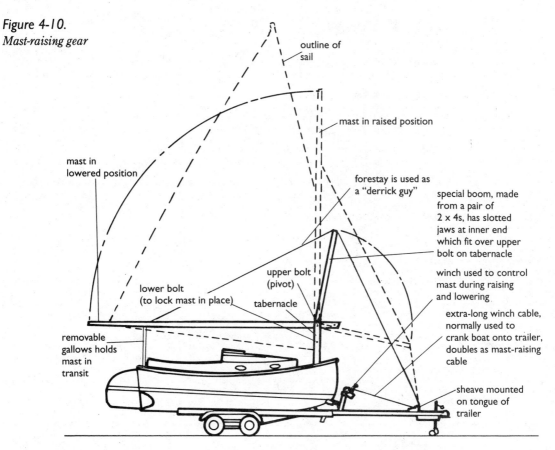

outline of
sail

mast in raised position

mast in
lowered position

forestay is used as
a "derrick guy"

special boom, made
from a pair of
2 x 4s, has slotted
jaws at inner end
which fit over upper
bolt on tabernacle

upper bolt
(pivot)

winch used to control
mast during raising
and lowering

lower bolt
(to lock mast in place)

tabernacle

extra-long winch cable,
normally used to
crank boat onto trailer,
doubles as mast-raising
cable

removable
gallows holds
mast in
transit

sheave mounted
on tongue of
trailer

Figure 4-11.
Built-in storage box

box can be fitted anywhere
it doesn't interfere with
boat handling; mounting
brackets may be welded
or bolted to
trailer frame

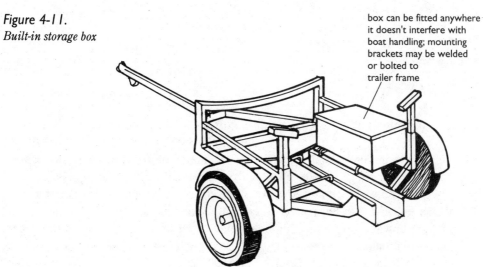

Trailer Walkways

Walkways are handy if you don't want to get your feet wet and your ramp technique calls for submerging the trailer fairly deeply and then walking out onto it to, say, snap on or unsnap the winch cable from the bow eye. You can buy fancy galvanized steel step-plates that bolt into the trailer frame (Wesbar sells 9½-inch-wide by 36-inch-long platforms — shown in Figure 4-12 — for $32 each) or you can simply use a wood 2 x 6 or 2 x 8 (the width depending on how good your balance is) held on by a couple of U-bolts to serve the same purpose. If you opt for walkways, try to install them so they won't get in the way when you're applying bottom paint to your boat in the spring — or be sure they're easily removable when painting time comes.

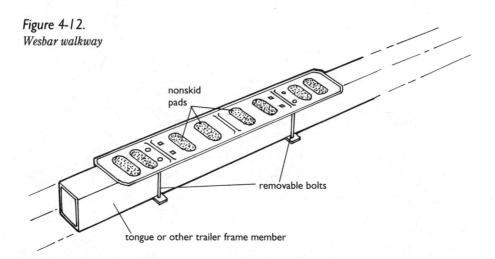

Figure 4-12.
Wesbar walkway

nonskid
pads

removable bolts

tongue or other trailer frame member

Guide Bars

Side-mounted guide bars, shown in Figure 3-1, help you to center your boat on her trailer as she is retrieved at a ramp. They are especially useful where the aft end of the trailer is totally submerged, making it difficult to judge the correct approach direction. They're also handy when retrieving a boat in choppy water or crosswinds. Most guide bars are made either of PVC (polyvinyl chloride plastic) or steel, with rollers or padding to prevent scuffing the boat. Some models include brackets to mount lights, keeping them up high and out of the water. Many boat people prefer steel guide bars to the plastic variety, as they are sturdier for use in adverse wind and wave conditions.

Trailer Locks

An ordinary padlock can be run through the hole in a lever-type coupler latch (Figure 11-1) to secure a parked trailer — or you can buy one of a variety of special locks to serve the same purpose. Both trailer dealers and hardware stores can supply you.

Special Lights and Reflectors

These aids to visibility, above and beyond what's legally required for highway travel, may also be useful when loading at a ramp at night. A new offering from Wesbar turns a boat trailer into the nautical equivalent of an airport runway by providing a string of truly waterproof lights, operated from the tow vehicle's electrical system, along each side of the trailer bed even if it's underwater. You just aim the boat at the "runway" and go. The lights can also be used for roadside emergencies when extra lighting around the boat is needed. What will they think of next?

PART TWO

How to Pick the Right Tow Vehicle

CHAPTER FIVE.

What Makes a
Good Tow Vehicle?

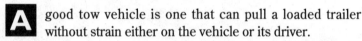 good tow vehicle is one that can pull a loaded trailer without strain either on the vehicle or its driver.

Most car and truck manufacturers specify the maximum towing capacity for each of their vehicles. But how are these ratings figured? Is it just a matter of engine displacement and maybe vehicle weight, or is it more complicated?

It's more complicated — a lot more complicated — than that. A quick glance at some of the vehicle towing capacity ratings in Appendix 2 will show that neither the curb weight of the vehicle nor its engine size is the main determinant of towing capacity. Nor is the primary factor in rating towing capacity the car's horsepower, or whether it has front-wheel rather than rear-wheel drive.

In fact, a vehicle's capacity to tow a trailer depends on a *combination* of more than a dozen different elements. The following is a list of these rating factors — variables the car makers think about before assigning ratings for a vehicle's maximum towing capacity.

Car Weight

The weight of the tow vehicle affects steering as well as load-carrying capacity. The rule of thumb used to be: Don't tow a loaded trailer heavier than your car. Weight is still a factor in determining towing capacity, but not as pronounced as it was a few years ago. For example, some cars listed in Appendix 2 have trailer weight limits as small as 25% of curb weight (weight of the car with full fuel tank but no occupants or luggage) or even less, while others are rated to tow significantly more than their own weight.

Rear Suspension Strength

Overload springs, load levelers, heavy-duty shock absorbers, and other such additions (usually offered as optional extras rather than as standard features) can help a tow car accept bigger loads.

Trailer Towing Package Options

Adding a factory-installed trailer towing package specifically designed by the manufacturer to improve a vehicle's towing capability can improve maximum towing capacity no end. In fact, these package options often can be the biggest single influence on rated tow-vehicle capacity. Take for example the little Volvo 240, weighing in at 2,985 pounds. With no trailer towing package, it's rated to tow 2,000 pounds. Add the optional tow package, consisting mainly of an automatic transmission fluid (ATF) cooler, and the tow-capacity rating rises to 3,300 pounds — more than the vehicle weight itself.

What's in a towing package? The specific items vary from make to make, but an unusually complete trailer towing package might include the following components:

- Heavy-duty radiator
- Heavy-duty transmission or transaxle oil cooler
- Heavy-duty turn signals
- Special trailer towing suspension, front and rear
- Dual exhaust system to boost horsepower
- Factory-installed frame hitch
- Heavy-duty signal flasher
- Auxiliary power steering fluid cooler
- Heavy-duty engine oil cooler
- Higher-ratio axle gearing
- Heavy-duty front brakes
- Heavy-duty wide tires
- Larger U-joint
- High-amp alternator
- Heavy-duty battery
- Factory-installed trailer wiring harness, including take-outs and relays for trailer lights, battery recharging (for house trailers), electric trailer brakes, and both halves of a weatherproof connector plug with pigtails to hook up to a trailer.

Factory-packaged systems can be extensive — but at a typical cost of $300 to $500, not expensive, considering what you get.

On the other hand, retrofitting an existing vehicle with the same equipment can set you back several thousand dollars, especially if you pay a mechanic to do the job rather than do it yourself. And most retrofit jobs aren't easy. Oil coolers, transmission fluid coolers, supplemental engine coolant radiators, heavy-duty suspension, higher-ratio axle gearing — all are available as "kits" in the auto aftermarket. If you install only one or two components to correct a specific problem — such as overheating in hilly terrain — the cost may be justifiable. But usually the best economic choice is to trade up to a vehicle already equipped to do the job.

Suitability of Hitch Attachment Points

Certain cars have easy-to-bolt-on hitches that can be obtained through trailer retailers from aftermarket suppliers like Hitch World (a U-Haul subsidiary), Reese, Draw-Tite, or Da'Lan (a foreign car and truck hitch specialist). Other cars won't fit any off-the-shelf hitches known to man. If you happen to own one of these "nothing fits" automobiles, you may have a problem with no easy solution. In some cases (such as with the 1989 Jeep Cherokee) the only right way is to order the hitch to be factory-installed when the car is built. To be safe, check hitch requirements and availability before you buy your new tow vehicle.

Incidentally, unless you want to risk voiding your auto warranty, forget using a bumper hitch on any new car. Before the days of shock-absorbing bumpers, bumper hitches were extensively used for light and medium loads, since they were easy to install and inexpensive. But today such hitches are not recommended except for the very lightest loads, and in several states *all* bumper hitches are banned.

Truck hitches are something else again; "step hitches" mounted on a step at the center of the bumper of many light trucks are not considered bumper hitches in the usual sense.

Suitable Trailer Hitch and Ball Configuration

Hitch and ball size and type vary according to the size and type of load to be towed. See Figure 3-17 for the classifications you can choose from, and see Chapter 7 for a discussion of the wide variety of hitch and ball types available.

Wheelbase

Length between front and rear wheels affects steering and traction. The longer the wheelbase, the better for towing, all other things being equal. Example: A heavy tongue weight on a short-wheelbase vehicle such as a Honda Civic (not recommended for towing) can wreck the car's handling characteristics.

High Engine Power and Torque at Relatively Low RPM

Any tow vehicle's engine should have sufficient horsepower and torque to accelerate promptly when entering a highway and to climb the steepest hills expected to be encountered without having to reduce speed excessively. Power should be obtainable at moderate engine speeds to avoid constant downshifting. That usually means having an engine that derives extra power from a large cylinder displacement, rather than a turbocharger to boost power. In fact, some manufacturers (e.g. Saab and Chrysler) recommend against using turbocharged engines on tow vehicles.

Rear-Wheel Versus Front-Wheel Drive

FWD cars have more weight on the front wheels and less on the back wheels compared with RWD cars. And weight distribution — how the car weight and the tongue weight are distributed between front and rear wheels — affects traction, steering, and ability of the car to absorb the extra load of the trailer. With typical vehicle weight on the back wheels of only 36 or 37% for FWD vehicles (vs. 44 or 45% for RWD models), the FWD cars have less traction to pull big loads, especially on steep grades (such as launching ramps) where weight distribution is shifted off the front wheels and onto the back ones. It's largely for this reason that Chrysler Corporation rates even most of its big cars to tow a maximum of only 2,000 pounds.

Drive Gear Ratio

The so-called axle ratio (i.e. the number of engine revolutions made for each revolution of the drive wheels) affects rear-wheel torque: The higher the ratio, the faster the engine is turning for a given road speed, and the higher the torque. Higher ratios give greater pep and pulling power, but poorer gas economy.

Cooling Capacity

ATF (automatic transmission fluid), transaxle lube, power steering fluid, engine oil, engine coolant — all can heat up more than usual when subjected to the adverse conditions of towing a heavy trailer. Manufacturers of vehicles designed for such heavy-duty conditions offer special cooling equipment as options.

Brake Capacity

Some cars have higher-capacity brakes than others, and vehicles towing big loads may need trailer brakes to help control the combined moving mass of both vehicles. Most states require trailer brakes for loads over 3,000 pounds (see Appendix 1). But five states — and many automakers — require trailer brakes on some models for loads over a piddling 1,000 pounds.

Heavy-Duty Tires

Fat and thick tires with a wide tread area provide not only better traction, but a margin of safety where heavy loads are involved. They're recommended for towing by some manufacturers, required by others.

Possible Manufacturer's Liability

Some car makers seem more sensitive than others to the possibility of lawsuits if something should go wrong while one of their cars is towing a trailer. I asked one corporate auto marketer whose cars seemed to be at least the equal of other brands rated for 1,000 to 2,000 pounds why his weren't recommended for towing at all. "In this day and age," he responded, "the whole hang-up is liability. We may change our minds later, but for now, we just don't want to take a chance."

The moral of this story is that, if you try towing a trailer without first checking your owner's manual and warranty, you could be in for big trouble. With the new closer-to-the-limit car designs, car makers say that towing a load that's too heavy might overheat and consequently damage engine, transmission, and brakes, and could overstress tires, damage suspension, cause steering problems, or scrape the muffler and rear end as the car bottoms out on the road. And low-powered engines might mean having to slow down on grades to the point that the car's a menace to traffic.

How can you avoid the problems of towing with an underrated vehicle? First figure out how much load you have to tow. The tables in Chapter 3 will give you an approximate gross trailer weight for various boat lengths. But note: These are just guidelines. Your boat and trailer weights are likely to vary from these figures; better check your registration papers or sales literature for exact numbers. And don't forget to add a couple of hundred pounds for miscellaneous gear stowed aboard the boat while trailering.

Then consult Appendix 2 to find which cars are rated to tow how big a load, and which are not recommended for *any* towing. Caution: The list covers most makes and models, including vans and pickup trucks, but is not complete. Check your vehicle dealer if you can't find the machine you're looking for in Appendix 2.

Finally, be sure to use a car that's fully suited to the towing task at hand, as determined by the people who should know — the manufacturers. Judging from my experience, you can't always rely on what the salesman says. In researching the data for Appendix 2, for example, I was given incorrect tow rating information by five different sales and customer service representatives for five different vehicle brands.

Consequently, your best bet is to check the manufacturer's literature rather than just asking the salesman. You'll almost always find detailed trailer towing information in the owner's manual (usually available for study in the showroom simply for the asking), if it's not spelled out in the usual sales brochures on the racks in the showroom.

In summary: These days you can't assume that any heavy car with a big engine is suitable to tow a trailer. There are many factors beyond weight and power that affect towing capacity. But if you use care and diligence in picking your new tow car, you'll get years of boat-trailering pleasure in return.

CHAPTER SIX.

Two Dozen Good
Choices for a
Tow Vehicle

A s you may already know, finding a good tow vehicle to suit your needs can be difficult. In my survey of 1991 vehicle trailer-towing capabilities in Appendix 2, more than 30% of over 100 passenger-car makes and models I checked out are not recommended for *any* towing, and only 13 are rated to tow even as much as 3,000 pounds. Vans and sports utility vehicles (as opposed to out-and-out commercial vehicles such as pickup trucks) fared a little better: Of 36 models surveyed, 23 (64%) could pull 3,000 pounds or more.

To make it easier for you to choose a good trailer-towing vehicle, Figure 6-1 focuses on the two dozen vehicles (excluding pickups) with the biggest towing capacity — at least 4,500 pounds (the weight of a typical open 21-foot powerboat and gear loaded on a trailer).

Data are given for capacity in terms of *trailer* load. You should know, however, that some vehicle makers also place a ceiling on the combined weight of the *towing vehicle plus the loaded trailer* (officially called GCWR or "gross combined weight rating"). In such cases the manufacturer is, in effect, placing a limit on the allowable weight of passengers, luggage, and other "payload" in the *towing* vehicle. Usually the specified GCWR is great enough so that limiting it is not a problem for trailer boaters. But occasionally it can cut into the allowable combined weight of boat and trailer significantly.

To take one example: Jeep specifies a maximum GCWR of 9,060 pounds for its Wagoneer Limited (discontinued in 1991). Since the curb weight of this vehicle is 3,467 pounds, if the towed load is assumed to be right at the maximum of

Figure 6-1.

Two dozen good tow car choices

Make and Model	Towing Capacity (lbs.)	Wheelbase (rounded; in inches)	Approx. 1991 Base Sticker Price
Passenger cars			
Buick Roadmaster Wagon	5,000	116	$18,000
Cadillac Brougham	5,000	122	28,000
Chevy Caprice V8	5,000	116	16,000
Ford Cr. Victoria	5,000	114	18,000
Lincoln Town Car	5,000	117	28,000
Olds Custom Cruiser	5,000	116	18,000
Minivans *(curb weight under 4,000 lbs.)*			
Ford Aerostar	4,900	119	14,000
Mazda MPV	4,500	110	15,000
Full-sized vans *(curb weight 4,000 lbs. or higher)*			
Chevrolet Astro	6,000	111	$15,000
Chevrolet Sportvan	10,000	125	15,000
Dodge B350 Wagon	8,600	128	14,400
Ford E-250 Wagon	10,000	138	14,800
Small Sports Utility Vehicles *(SUVs) (curb weight under 4,000 lbs.)*			
Chevy S-10 Blazer	6,000	101	$13,000
Ford Explorer	5,700	102	15,000
Jeep Cherokee 4x4	5,000	104	16,000
Mazda Navajo	5,000	102	18,000
Olds Bravada	5,500	107	24,000
Full-sized SUVs *(curb weight 4,000 lbs. or higher)*			
Chevy Blazer	6,000	107	$17,000
Chevy Suburban	9,500	130	16,000
Dodge Ramcharger	7,500	106	16,000
Ford Bronco	7,800	105	17,000
Jeep Grand Wagoneer	5,000	109	28,000
Range Rover	5,500	100	36,000
Toyota Land Cruiser	5,000	112	22,000

Note: Only passenger cars, vans, and sports utility vehicles (SUVs) rated to tow 4,500 or more pounds are listed here. For pickup trucks and other commercial-type vehicles, see Appendix 2-B.

5,000 pounds, the sum of empty Wagoneer and loaded trailer is 8,467 pounds. That leaves only 593 pounds for passengers and gear — less than four 150 pound people traveling without luggage.

To supplement the data given in Appendix 2 for these vehicles, Figure 6-1 also indicates wheelbase (the longer the better for towing), and approximate base list price (as a rough indicator only, subject to additions for optional extras, freight, and other charges, and subtractions for discounts, rebates, and other credits). Check — and bargain with — local dealers for actual prices.

Serious shoppers will also want to evaluate factors such as car-like comfort, ride, and "feel"; styling; interior roominess and cargo-carrying capacity; relative ease of parking and garageability; and fuel economy.

Not included in the list of "good choices" are any older models, particularly cars built in the days before front-wheel drives, lightweight chassis, and smaller engines took over a major share of the market. Many of these beefier, more powerful golden oldies — specifically passenger cars over 12 years or so old — offer a nice combination of relatively low cost and good towing ability, and you may decide that one of these ancient monsters is just what you need. But there are enough obvious drawbacks to owning such vehicles in terms of maintenance and style to justify excluding them from further discussion here.

Doing your "homework" before deciding which make and model to buy is no easy task. The information in Figure 6-1 and Appendix 2 is designed to save you hours, even days, in your quest. Happy shopping!

PART THREE

How to Set Up and Use Your Trailer and Tow Vehicle

CHAPTER SEVEN.

Setting Up a New Trailer and Tow Vehicle

You may be chafing at the bit to pile the boat on the trailer, hitch up, and take off for the nearest launching ramp. If you've already adjusted the trailer to fit the boat, complied with all legal requirements for trailers in your travel area, determined that the towed weight and tongue weight are suitable for your tow vehicle, set up your rig to minimize road instability and sway, made a pre-tow safety inspection, and learned how to drive safely with a long, wide, heavy load at your stern ... well, then, go right ahead. Otherwise, you may save yourself a heap of trouble by first reading the rest of this and the next two chapters.

Adjusting Your New Trailer to Fit Your Boat

Trailers have a lot of in-and-out and up-and-down adjustment points. Here are step-by-step directions on how to use them so your boat is properly supported for smooth and damage-free towing.

1. Position the Boat at the Correct Balance Point

Most trailers balance well when trailer tongue weight — the downward force exerted by the trailer on the hitch — is around 7 to 8% of the loaded trailer weight. You'll need to know your loaded trailer weight in order to choose the right equipment for your rig (see Chapter 3). If you don't know either the boat weight (with engine and gear) or the empty trailer weight, you can check your boat sales brochure and the required tag on the starboard side of the trailer frame. If neither a brochure nor a tag is available, you can make a weight estimate using Figures 3-5, 3-6, and 3-7, or you can weigh the trailer-and-boat combination on a truck scale. Check building supply yards or call your favorite local trucking firm to find one in your area.

If your loaded rig weighs 4,200 pounds or less, you can measure actual tongue weight using an ordinary bathroom scale, which typically reads up to 300 pounds (4,200 x 7% = 294 pounds). Simply place the scale on the pavement under the tongue. Be sure the surface under the scale is flat and level; otherwise the reading will not be accurate. You can set the scale on a piece of plywood if you can't find a patch of flat pavement. Lift or lower the tongue so the trailer frame is horizontal (especially important with tandem trailers), insert a spacer such as a wood 2 x 4 vertically between scale and tongue coupler, and read the scale. (If you don't have any short scraps of 2 x 4, you may want to acquire a couple; they may come in handy later as wheel chocks, jack basepad, etc.) It will probably be necessary to move the boat back and forth using trial and error until you get the right tongue weight. If the tongue weight is greater than your scale's capacity, you can use the rig in Figure 7-1 to bring it within range. For a truly accurate reading, you'll need to measure the lever arm distances precisely — and for the ultimate in precision, don't forget to subtract the scale reading for the 2 x 4 without the tongue weight resting on it.

2. Check to be Sure the
Boat is Well Supported

Check all bunks and rollers — especially keel rollers, if the boat has them — to be sure all contribute their share of support to the load, and that the hull isn't

Figure 7-1.
Weighing a heavy trailer tongue

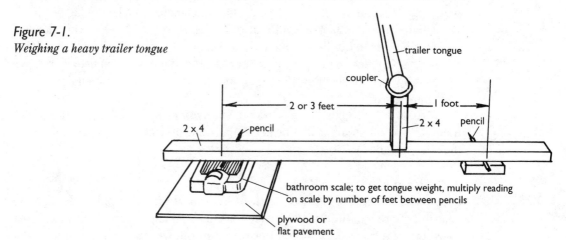

being deformed at any support point. (Where keel rollers are used, generally they support most of the load, and side rollers or bunks are adjusted just snug enough to prevent hull sway when on the road.) Adjust each support point up or down as necessary. Bunks, if used, should project beyond the transom at least an inch or two, so that the transom is fully supported, particularly if most or all of the engine weight is concentrated at the stern. This will help prevent distortion of the hull skin near the transom, especially if the boat is stored on her trailer for long periods of time.

If you have an all-roller trailer, the aftermost set of support rollers should be placed as close under the transom as possible for the same reason. If the last rollers extend beyond the transom, however, they may hinder backward movement of the boat on a ramp.

If you need to raise the boat temporarily to make these adjustments, you can often do so using a small hydraulic jack and wood shores (e.g. more scrap 2 x 4s), and bracing against part of the trailer frame or the pavement below. Sometimes the easiest way to snug rollers against the hull is to loosen the securing bolts only partially, then tap the roller or bunk assembly with a small sledge hammer. A 3-pound sledge with a 10-inch handle has enough heft to move most supports.

If the trailer dimensions are such that when the boat is well supported, the tongue weight is either too heavy or too light, all is not lost. Most trailers have two or more axle positions (some have eight or ten), so you can slide the whole trailer bed forward or aft relative to the axle to suit the size and shape of the load.

If you have to slide the axle along the bed, it may be easiest to remove the boat first. If you have a small, manhandleable boat or access to a boat hoist (such as is available at many yacht clubs and some marinas), you can simply lift the boat off and set it on cushions or a soft grassy spot on the ground. Otherwise, getting the boat off the trailer before it's fitted to be used at a launching ramp can be a chore. If your trailer has a lot of rollers and they turn freely when loaded, you may be able to tilt the bed aft and ease the boat back with the winch, sliding her off the back end onto a grassy or padded area. If not, you can usually remove the boat by systematically inching it off, using jacks, wood props, cinder blocks, and elbow grease.

If removing the boat seems too difficult, you can try jacking up the trailer frame at several strategically located points and moving the axle position with the boat *in situ*.

3. Position the Winch Stand

Leaving all bolts just tight enough to keep parts from slipping during the adjustment procedure, place the winch stand in its approximate position. Then move the winch and bow stop up or down on the winch stand until the winch cable or strap leads horizontally to the boat's bow eye without interfering with the bow stop. Be sure the vee-shaped bow stop fits firmly against the boat's stem.

4. Remeasure Tongue Weight to Check that it's Still in the Right Range

If it's not, make appropriate adjustments until it is. Then tighten all nuts and bolts (preferably with a socket or box wrench, to avoid stripping the corners off the heads), and the job is done.

Make Sure Your Lights Work

Most new trailers come with lights already installed and a four-prong connector at the coupling ready to plug into a mating connector at the back end of the tow vehicle. If you're all set with lights and wiring on both trailer and car, and have tested them to make sure they work, you can skip this section. Otherwise, here are some tips on how to set up a trailer lighting system.

Hook up Lights

Refer to the schematic wiring diagram in Figure 7-2. Note that there is a more or less standard color scheme for trailer wiring: brown for taillights, side marker lights, and identification light bar; yellow for left turn signal and brake light; green for right turn signal and brake light; and white for ground. If you use this wiring scheme, you can interchange with other trailers and tow vehicles and your lights, in most cases, will work without needing any adjustments. For what to do if they *don't* work, see Chapter 12.

Use Top-Quality Wire and Plugs

If you buy a trailer wiring harness and mating trailer-to-vehicle connector plugs (available at marine supply stores and mail-order houses as well as at trailer and hitch dealers), be sure they use high-quality materials. Look for shiny golden-yellow all-copper wire; some cheap wiring is aluminum or some other hard-to-solder material. The thicker the wire and its insulation, the less trouble you'll have with breaking, chafing, and shorting out.

Make Good Ground Connections

Some wiring setups attach the ground wire lead from the tow vehicle to the front end of the trailer, and the ground leads from the taillights to the rear end of the trailer, and use the steel frame of the trailer as the intermediate conductor. This configuration often causes trouble. If the frame has a tilt bed, any electricity flowing between the front and back ends of the trailer has to pass through the pivot point between the two halves, and often this path is blocked by road grime, rust,

Figure 7-2.
Schematic wiring diagram

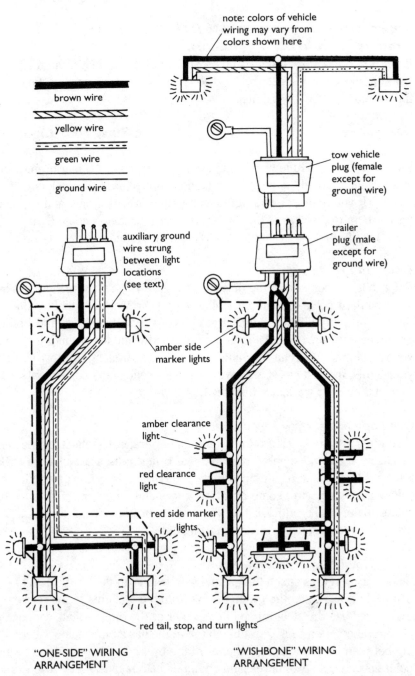

note: colors of vehicle
wiring may vary from
colors shown here

brown wire

yellow wire

green wire

ground wire

tow vehicle
plug (female
except for
ground wire)

trailer
plug (male
except for
ground wire)

auxiliary ground
wire strung
between light
locations
(see text)

amber side
marker lights

amber clearance
light

red clearance
light

red side marker
lights

red tail, stop, and turn lights

"ONE-SIDE" WIRING
ARRANGEMENT

"WISHBONE" WIRING
ARRANGEMENT

or paint. And after the trailer has started to rust, the connections between wiring and the trailer steel are apt to deteriorate. In fact, a poor ground connection is the number one cause of trailer light failure.

To avoid problems with a faulty ground, run a separate ground wire along the trailer frame and connect it to all ground terminal points at both front and rear.

Make Sure all Wire Splices are Tight and Permanent

If you just twist two wires together to join them, wrap the joint with electrical tape, and forget it, you're almost sure to have an electrical failure eventually. The same is true if you use household-type "wire taps," those cone-shaped plastic connectors (Figure 7-3) commonly used in household wall switches. In a marine

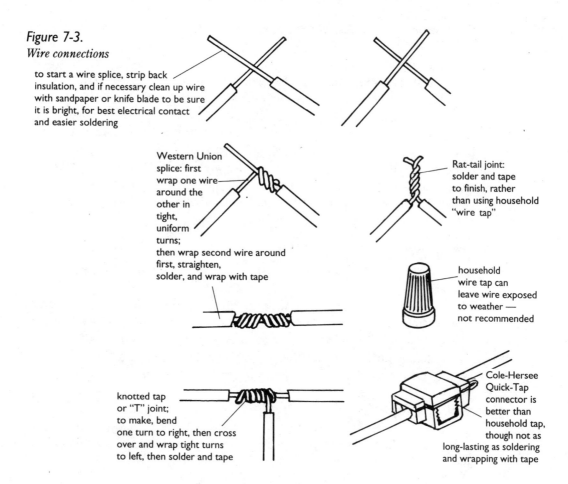

Figure 7-3.
Wire connections

to start a wire splice, strip back insulation, and if necessary clean up wire with sandpaper or knife blade to be sure it is bright, for best electrical contact and easier soldering

Western Union splice: first wrap one wire around the other in tight, uniform turns; then wrap second wire around first, straighten, solder, and wrap with tape

Rat-tail joint: solder and tape to finish, rather than using household "wire tap"

household wire tap can leave wire exposed to weather — not recommended

knotted tap or "T" joint; to make, bend one turn to right, then cross over and wrap tight turns to left, then solder and tape

Cole-Hersee Quick-Tap connector is better than household tap, though not as long-lasting as soldering and wrapping with tape environment (and particularly in salt water), the copper conductor oxidizes and, if alloyed with zinc or tin, may be electrolyzed to a soft, pulpy mess. If you want a really good connection, you must strip the insulation back an inch or so from the end of each wire, tightly twist together the wires to be joined (as in Figure 7-3), coat the twisted pair with solder, and cover with two layers of electrical tape. Even then, you may have to resplice every few years.

Easier and quicker than soldering but not quite so long-lasting are the plastic squeeze-together wire splicers such as Cole-Hersee's Quick-Tap connectors (Figure 7-3). If you use these, the electrical flow will last longer if you seal around the ends with silicone sealant.

Make Frequent Lighting
System Inspections
Regular maintenance is a must. See Chapter 11 for step-by-step instructions.

Get your Trailer Registered

All states require trailer licensing for travel on public roads. Be sure your trailer license plate is in place and properly lighted for night driving, and carry registration papers in your tow vehicle at all times.

A tip on attaching the license plate: Make it easy to remove, and take it off if you are leaving your trailer unattended for any length of time. Trailer license plates are a favorite target of waterfront thieves. Also, license plates on tilt-bed trailers are often mounted too low, so that when the bed is tilted, the license plate is crunched into the ramp pavement. If you have such an arrangement, you can keep your plate in one piece by removing it before launching. Just don't forget to replace it before heading back on the highway.

What Other Equipment
and Papers do you Need?

If your boat is particularly long, wide, or high, you may need special materials such as "overwide" permits and additional safety gear to travel on the highway. There's also the matter of liability insurance required in some states. And if you're thinking of towing two trailers in tandem, you'll need to study the rules for your area. A state-by-state summary appears in Appendix 1.

Pick the Right Hitch and Ball

If your tow vehicle doesn't already have one, you'll need to buy a hitch and ball and either install them yourself or have it done for you.

Hitches, couplers, and balls all use the same capacity rating system as shown in Figure 3-4: Class I for towing loads up to 2,000 pounds, Class II for 2,000 to 3,500 pounds, Class III for 3,500 to 5,000 pounds, and Class IV for 5,000 to 10,000 pounds. There is also a "fifth-wheel" hitch that can be set into the bed of a truck over or forward of the rear wheels to carry even more weight than a Class IV frame hitch. But fifth-wheel hitches are for extremely large boats — and beyond the scope of this book.

I recommend installing a hitch that's strong enough to match or exceed the manufacturer's rated maximum towing capacity for your vehicle. That way, if you move up in boat size before you replace the vehicle, you won't be forced to replace your frame hitch.

The strength of a frame hitch depends not only on its material and construction but also on the strength of the tow vehicle body and frame. Smaller hitches sometimes attach to the back bumper as well as to the frame, immobilizing the so-called crash-resistant or "5-mph" bumper and thus preventing the slight yielding on impact that is designed to help protect the vehicle body. If that's the only type of hitch that will fit your vehicle, you have no choice, but it's better to use a frame-only hitch, so the bumper can function in collisions as it was designed to do.

If you opt for a small, lightweight Class I hitch (perhaps out of necessity if you have a small, lightweight car), you may be able to bolt it on yourself. Heavy-duty hitches are more complicated and difficult to attach, so if you're thinking of a big hitch, I recommend hiring a commercial hitch installer to do the job. U-Haul, the nation's biggest hitch installer, can do it for you; so can any dealer for Eaz-Lift, Draw-Tite, Reese, Da'Lan, or one of a number of other hitch manufacturers. You can get addresses and telephone numbers for dealers in your area by calling the corporate numbers listed in Appendix 3, or you can try your own auto mechanic. It's likely to be quicker and maybe safer to use someone who specializes in hitches.

I recommend buying a receiver-type hitch (Figure 7-4) rather than a fixed-platform type (Figure 7-5), even for light-duty service. With the receiver type, you can remove the ball platform or "hitch bar" (also sometimes called the "drawbar") and store it inside the vehicle when not in use. That keeps it out of the weather, forestalls rust, and prevents theft of your ball (another favorite target of waterfront thieves). Moreover, if you're a certified boat nut like me and have two or more trailers with different sized couplers (such as a 1⅞-inch size on one trailer and a 2-inch size on another), and perhaps different hitch height requirements as well, you can carry a variety of ball/platform combinations to suit your changing needs.

There are several ways to adjust hitch ball height after your frame hitch is installed, so that your boat and trailer will ride on the level rather than bow-up or

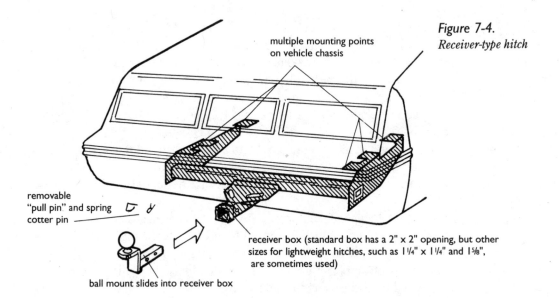

multiple mounting points
on vehicle chassis

Figure 7-4.
Receiver-type hitch

removable
"pull pin" and spring
cotter pin

receiver box (standard box has a 2" x 2" opening, but other
sizes for lightweight hitches, such as 1¼" x 1¼" and 1⅝",
are sometimes used)

ball mount slides into receiver box

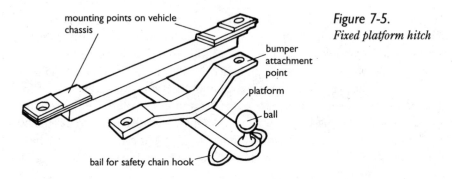

mounting points on vehicle
chassis

bumper
attachment
point

platform

ball

Figure 7-5.
Fixed platform hitch

bail for safety chain hook

bow-down. To raise or lower the ball on the tow vehicle, you can (1) try replacing the frame hitch with a lower or higher one (not usually a practical option; most hitches for a given vehicle will be about the same height); (2) use a "high lift" ball (Figure 7-6) to change the ball height of an existing hitch; or (3) in conjunction with a receiver-type hitch, use a "step-up," "step-down," or "two-way" ball mount (Figure 7-7) to adjust the ball height. That way you can change the height of your ball by 1 to 6 inches or more. A fourth option is to use a step-up coupler on the trailer (Figure 7-8), which works well when towing with, say, a high-chassis truck or SUV.

Figure 7-6.
Types of hitch balls

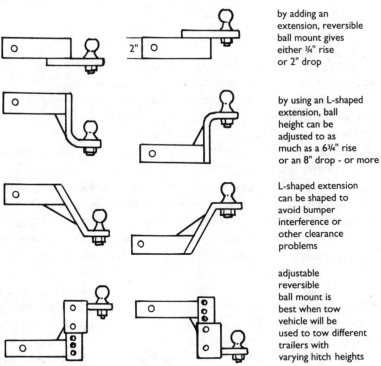

solid ball

two-piece ball

lift

lift

mounting shank

lock washer (very important)

A   B   C   D   E

A. Standard heavy-duty ball. Note wide neck.
B. Standard light- or medium-duty ball. Note narrower neck.
C. "High lift" ball raises coupler 1".

D. Taller "high lift" ball raises coupler 2". Note heavier mounting shank. Shanks come in ¾", 1", and 1¼" diameters.
E. Two-piece ball - not recommended except for lightest loads.

Figure 7-7.
Reversible ball mounts

2"

by adding an extension, reversible ball mount gives either ¾" rise or 2" drop

by using an L-shaped extension, ball height can be adjusted to as much as a 6¾" rise or an 8" drop - or more

L-shaped extension can be shaped to avoid bumper interference or other clearance problems

adjustable reversible ball mount is best when tow vehicle will be used to tow different trailers with varying hitch heights

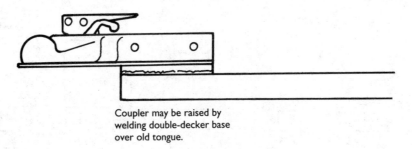

Figure 7-8.
Step-up coupler

Coupler may be raised by
welding double-decker base
over old tongue.

There are some special-purpose hitches and hitch attachments that you may find useful to know about, as follows.

Step bumper hitches (Figure 7-9) are sometimes mounted on the rear bumpers of pickup trucks. Sometimes the standard step bumper is comparatively light-duty (under 1,000 pounds of towing capacity or even less), and an optional, beefed-up bumper may be ordered to increase trailer towing capacity.

The unique and clever *PullRite hitch* (Figure 7-10) is made to fit most pickup trucks and vans. One model tows up to 10,000 pounds; another will handle up to 20,000 pounds. According to the company (address in Appendix 3), this hitch combines the benefits of a big-truck fifth wheel (minimized sway problems, easy hookup, great maneuverability, short turning radius) without the drawbacks (lost cargo space, high cost), and also gives better handling and other benefits.

Weight-distributing hitches, also known as *load-equalizing hitches* (Figure 7-11) spread out the tongue weight so it's shared by all trailer and tow vehicle wheels rather than concentrated mainly on the tow vehicle's rear wheels. This results in better steering and on-the-road stability and virtually eliminates rear-end sag. Some towing experts recommend weight-distributing hitches only for relatively big loads (4,000 or 5,000 pounds and upward). Others (including many

Figure 7-9.
Step bumper hitch

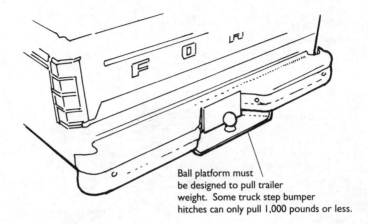

Ball platform must
be designed to pull trailer
weight. Some truck step bumper
hitches can only pull 1,000 pounds or less.

Figure 7-10.
PullRite hitch

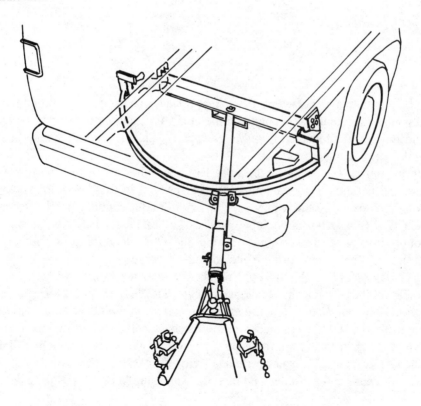

Figure 7-11.
Weight-distributing hitch

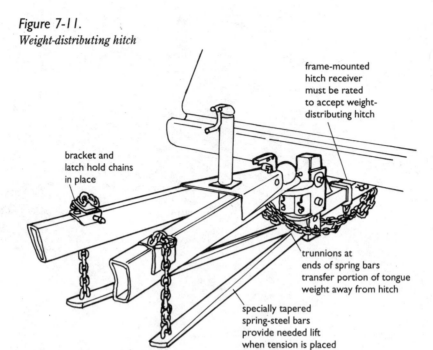

frame-mounted
hitch receiver
must be rated
to accept weight-
distributing hitch

bracket and
latch hold chains
in place

trunnions at
ends of spring bars
transfer portion of tongue
weight away from hitch

specially tapered
spring-steel bars
provide needed lift
when tension is placed
on chains

U.S. automotive manufacturers) say that a load-equalizing hitch is required for anything exceeding 2,000 pounds. Still others (including a number of Japanese and European automakers) don't recommend using weight-distributing hitches under any circumstances.

If your trailer load is significantly depressing the rear end of your tow vehicle, and potential remedies mentioned elsewhere in this book don't work, a weight-distributing hitch may be your answer. But caution: As already mentioned, if your trailer is equipped with surge brakes, they may be partially or totally inactivated by a weight-distributing hitch, depending on the specific design of hitch. Check with the hitch manufacturer first.

Sway controllers (Figure 7-12) reduce the tendency of crosswinds to push a trailer off the tow vehicle's track, which can cause fishtailing and steering problems. They may also help if you experience sway due to some of the causes of on-the-road instability outlined later in this chapter. But rather than treating the symptom by installing a sway controller (which, like some weight-distributing hitches, can prevent proper operation of surge brakes), it's usually better to treat the root cause of the problem. Some suggestions for doing this are given below.

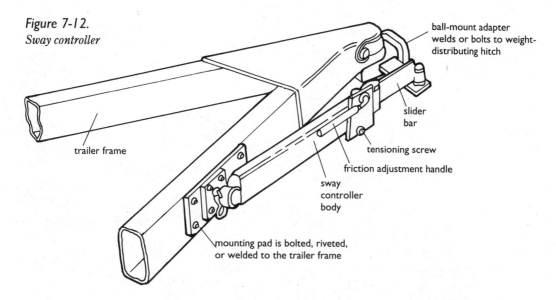

Figure 7-12.
Sway controller

ball-mount adapter welds or bolts to weight-distributing hitch

slider bar

trailer frame

tensioning screw

friction adjustment handle

sway controller body

mounting pad is bolted, riveted, or welded to the trailer frame

Plan Ahead to Minimize Instability While Towing

Some things seem to aggravate unstable behavior on the highway, such as fishtailing and sway. Here's a summary of the types of problems that can occur and how to deal with them. Some we've already mentioned; others we haven't.

Trailer Tongue Weight is too Light
Symptoms: Fishtailing and sway. *Solution*: Move trailer load forward on bed or move trailer axles aft until tongue weight is within proper range — usually 7 to 8% of gross trailer weight. Sometimes just rearranging the weight within the boat will help, such as moving luggage forward, filling or emptying water or fuel tanks, or even just pumping out the bilge.

Trailer Tongue Weight is too Heavy
Symptoms: The tow vehicle "squats," with its front end high and rear end low, making steering quirky and driving difficult. The tow vehicle may oversteer in turns, especially on downgrades. The trailer frame is lower forward than aft, so the hitch may bottom out on bumps. *Solution*: Move the center of gravity aft, using the same techniques as for a light tongue weight but in the opposite direction. If moving weight around isn't feasible, try using a weight-distributing hitch or installing heavier-duty rear suspension, pneumatic load-leveling shocks, helper springs (Figure 7-13), or adjustable pneumatic "load lifters" (Figure 7-14) on the tow vehicle.

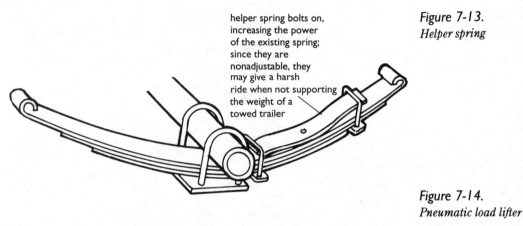

helper spring bolts on, increasing the power of the existing spring; since they are nonadjustable, they may give a harsh ride when not supporting the weight of a towed trailer

Figure 7-13.
Helper spring

Figure 7-14.
Pneumatic load lifter

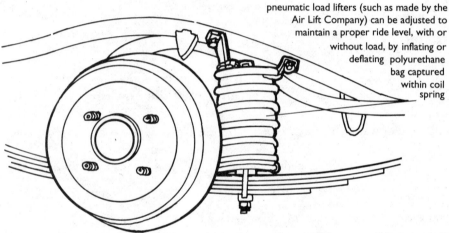

pneumatic load lifters (such as made by the Air Lift Company) can be adjusted to maintain a proper ride level, with or without load, by inflating or deflating polyurethane bag captured within coil spring

Trailer Tongue is too Short

Symptoms: Tracking is poor, with short, jerky, side-to-side movements. *Solution*: Lengthen the tongue. A trailer tongue is like a pendulum; the longer the pendulum arm, the slower the reaction to forces coming from the tow car or road. Some trailer manufacturers offer optional longer tongues. If yours doesn't, you can have a welder splice in an additional section on your existing tongue.

Trailer Load Center of Gravity (CG) is too High

Symptoms: Trailer sways, rolls from side to side, leans to the outside in turns. *Solution*: Find ways to reduce the height of the center of gravity of the load.

Trailer Frame is too Flexible

Symptoms: Trailer sways and may vibrate when towed; its frame may sag and twist under load, sometimes in an oscillating manner, leading to metal fatigue, cracks, and eventual frame failure. *Solution*: Be sure the frame is stiff enough to carry its intended load.

Trailer Suspension is too Soft

Symptoms: Trailer "bottoms out" on bumps (i.e. the axle hits the frame or the tires hit the fenders). Springs may fatigue and eventually break. If the trailer is frequently dunked in salt water, leaf springs may rust between the leaves to an extent great enough to reduce the leaf thickness and weaken the spring. *Solution*: Keep springs fully covered with a rust-inhibiting coating (paint or grease), and rinse with fresh water after every saltwater immersion. If necessary, replace springs with heavier-duty models, possibly with additional leaves.

Trailer Suspension Geometry is Wrong

Symptoms: In turns, trailer rolls to the outside, causing tow vehicle to want to turn sharper (oversteer). *Solution*: Depends on the specifics of the problem. For example, if the trailer is equipped with leaf springs and the pivoting shackles are at the front end, try moving them to the rear. If the trailer is a tandem model, the equalizer bars may be missing; be sure they are in place and functioning.

Trailer Tires are Underinflated

Symptoms: Trailer fishtails, sways, does not track well. *Solution:* In most cases all trailer tires should be inflated to the maximum pressure indicated on the sidewall. One exception: On tandem-axle trailers bothered by sway, sometimes reducing pressure in the front pair of tires by about 5 pounds below the maximum will help. But if you do this, more of the total load will be transferred to the rear tires; be sure they are rated to accept the added weight.

Trailer Tire Size is too Small or Tire Walls are too Weak for the Load Carried

Symptoms: The trailer will behave as if its tires are underinflated, even if they are pumped to maximum pressure. *Solution*: Replace the tires with larger, stronger, higher-capacity models. Be sure to leave 3 or 4 inches of space between the tire and fender for spring travel. That may mean buying new fenders, which are available in the aftermarket in steel, aluminum, and fiberglass.

In addition to the above *trailer* instability problems, there is another group of instability problems associated specifically with *tow vehicles* on which:

- Wheel base is too short;
- There is too much weight over rear end;
- Tire inflation is too low;
- Rear tires are too soft compared with front tires;
- The tow vehicle CG is too high;
- Rear overhang is too long;
- Rear suspension is too soft;
- Vehicle tires are too narrow or small;
- Tire walls are not stiff enough.

The symptoms are erratic or hard-to-control steering; sway; difficulty in braking; and a tendency for the tow-vehicle driver to feel loss of control. The solution is, obviously, to avoid the causative problem or problems.

Finally, there is one problem of instability associated with the *combined* tow-vehicle/trailer system: the speed of the rig. At some critical speed — 45 to 65 mph is typical — instability begins to appear in otherwise reasonably stable systems. The solution is again obvious: Simply slow down until the symptoms disappear.

Checking Out the
Rig Before You Tow

Now the boat is on her trailer in your driveway and you're all packed up and ready to take off for the launching ramp. Or are you? To be safe, it's best to check out both the loaded trailer and the tow vehicle before you go. Here's a pre-tow inspection checklist you can use now — and every time you tow — to help ensure the safety and security of your rig and to minimize on-the-road problems.

On the Tow Vehicle . . . Under the Hood

- Check all fluid levels (oil, transmission fluid, battery water, power steering, windshield washer, etc.).
- Check to be sure radiator cap is seated tightly.
- Check that battery terminals are free of corrosion.
- Check radiator hoses for leaks and for pliability.
- Check fanbelt for tension and wear.
- Check condition of transmission fluid. If color is pinkish, fluid is okay; if brownish, it's time for servicing.
- Check air filter for dirt and date last replaced.

On the Tow Vehicle . . . Outside

- Check tire pressure and tread wear. Use the vehicle manufacturer's recommendations for inflation; rear tires usually should have more pressure than front tires when towing a heavy load.

- Check lights for burnt-out bulbs or cracked or broken lenses.
- Check that headlights aim downward despite weight at rear.
- Check blinker system after trailer lights are connected.
- Check road clearance under back bumper and hitch, especially if traveling on bumpy roads.
- Check fuel supply in tank. If towing conditions will be particularly onerous (hot or hilly), consider using higher-octane gasoline than usual to help prevent knocking.
- Check that the hitch ball is marked with a diameter matching the diameter of the trailer coupler.
- Check that the ball is wrench-tight against its lock washer.

On the Trailer and Boat

- Check all trailer lights for proper operation and broken lenses.
- Check the electric plug to be sure it is fully engaged. If wet weather is expected, wrap connector with a couple of turns of electrical tape to help keep it dry.
- Check the electric plug and surrounding wires to be sure they won't chafe or short out during journey.
- Check trailer tire tread wear and pressure. (Inflate to maximum as specified on sidewall.)
- Check wheel lugs for tightness; be sure none are missing.
- Check all bolts and nuts on trailer frame for tightness (at least once a year).
- Check that both safety chains are crisscrossed under the trailer tongue (which prevents tongue from dropping to the road if the coupler separates from the hitch ball), that they're securely hooked into the tow-vehicle hitch (Figure 8-1), and that there is enough slack to prevent binding in tight turns.
- Check hookup of breakaway lanyard if trailer is equipped with brakes; leave sufficient slack for tight turns.
- Check coupler to be sure locking lever is in "down" position, ball is properly locked to coupler, and safety pin or padlock is in place on locking lever.
- Check tongue jack to be sure it is in full "up" position and has been lubricated recently.
- Check to be sure removable dolly wheel and/or stabilizer jacks, if any, have been removed.

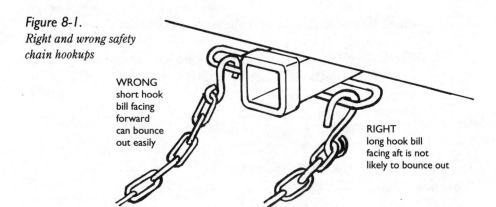

Figure 8-1.
Right and wrong safety
chain hookups

WRONG
short hook
bill facing
forward
can bounce
out easily

RIGHT
long hook bill
facing aft is not
likely to bounce out

- Check tilt-bed trailer pivot point to be sure locking pin is securely in place.
- Check load distribution to be sure tongue weight is within prescribed limits.
- Check to be sure trailer and tow vehicle are reasonably level when connected.
- Check tie-downs to be sure they are snug, well-tied, and properly padded at contact points with boat and trailer to prevent chafe.
- Check that boat's bow is securely held in place against the bow stop with at least two lines in addition to the winch line or cable. One of these lines will hold the bow forward against the stop, supplementing the winch line in case of breakage or inadvertent release. The other will hold the bow down against the trailer bed. For boats with extremely raked stems, a third line may be needed to keep the boat from sliding forward, up and over the bow stop, in the event of sudden, heavy braking.
- Check winch line or cable for chafe, fraying, etc.
- Check bow winch to be sure it has been lubricated recently.
- Check bow winch handle to be sure it's secure; if removable, take it off and stow it in the tow vehicle.
- Check rigging and gear on the boat to be sure nothing can come loose, flap, vibrate, or jiggle during the tow. Battery should be secured, canvas top folded down, etc.
- Check the boat's battery to be sure it's fully charged, especially if it will be needed for engine starting.

- Check engine prop to be sure there's sufficient road clearance below it.
- Check wheel bearings to be sure they are filled with grease.
- Check to be sure trailer spare tire is secure and usable.
- Check to be sure valid license plate is securely fastened in its proper place.

On the Tow Vehicle, in Passenger Compartment or Trunk

- Check that tow vehicle spare tire is in place and usable.
- Check to be sure that, if the spare tire is locked to the trailer frame with a padlock, you have the key.
- Check that a spare fuse for the tow vehicle lighting circuit, a spare flasher, and at least one spare bulb for each trailer light is aboard (and be familiar with how to install them).
- Check to be sure trailer registration (and vehicle registration) is on board.
- Check to be sure an appropriate toolkit is on board.

What's in an "Appropriate Toolkit?"

Here's a list:

- A lug wrench that fits the trailer wheel lugs. (Your car's lug wrench may not fit; better check to be sure.)
- A jack that's low-profile enough — and powerful enough — to be used under a trailer axle if the trailer has a flat tire. Small bottle-type hydraulic jacks are good for this purpose.
- A set of box wrenches and socket wrenches to fit all the bolts on the trailer.
- A set of screwdrivers to fit any screw on the trailer.
- A pair of locking-jaw pliers, such as the Vise-Grip brand, which can double as a wrench in a pinch and are handy for all kinds of other chores.
- A tire pressure gauge with a scale that reads higher than your trailer tires' maximum allowable pressure.
- An electrical repair kit including a wire stripper, electrical tape, clinch-type terminals, pliers, and a small voltmeter.

- A heavy (3-pound) hand sledge hammer to help adjust trailer components if they come loose.
- An assortment of short wood 2 x 4 scraps, including some wedge-shaped pieces that can double as wheel chocks.
- A grease gun loaded with premium-quality wheel-bearing grease.
- A roll of paper towels and "wash-and-wipe" moist towels for cleanup after messy emergency repairs.
- A bucket full of extra line for tie-downs and docking. Throw in a roll of duct tape to quiet rattles and keep small parts from vibrating loose.
- A pair of hip boots, a bathing suit, and/or a dry change of clothes. Even if launching and retrieving is ordinarily a dry-as-a-bone operation, you may someday run into a problem whose only solution involves getting wet.

Finished with the checkout? Great; now you're ready to roll.

CHAPTER NINE.
Trailer Towing and Handling

You may already be the world's greatest driver, but one thing is sure: With a trailer hitched to your tow vehicle's rear end, you'll need practice backing up. For room to perfect your technique, head for the nearest empty parking lot. Shopping center or school lots during off-hours make ideal practice sites.

Practice swinging around sharp corners without running the trailer wheels over the curb. You'll need to keep the tow vehicle going straight for a few more feet than you would without a trailer, then turn sharply into the corner. The trailer will follow right along.

The secret of good control while backing is to twist your upper body to the right so you're looking over your right shoulder out the rear window, down the centerline of the vehicle. That way it's much easier to visualize which way to turn the wheel to get the trailer to move where you want it.

Some folks recommend holding the steering wheel at the bottom. Then, they say, if you move your hand to the left, the trailer will back to the left, and if you move it to the right, the trailer will back to the right. But I find this procedure awkward, especially when I'm twisted around for a better view to the rear, and therefore I don't recommend it.

One more trick: When you have to back around a corner — whether into a driveway or to start down a launching ramp (Figure 9-1) — and you have a choice of which direction to approach from, start from the right (or what *would* be the right if you were facing the ramp or driveway) and back in a clockwise arc. That way it'll be easy to see the trailer's path out your driver's side window.

Figure 9-1.
Backing and turning

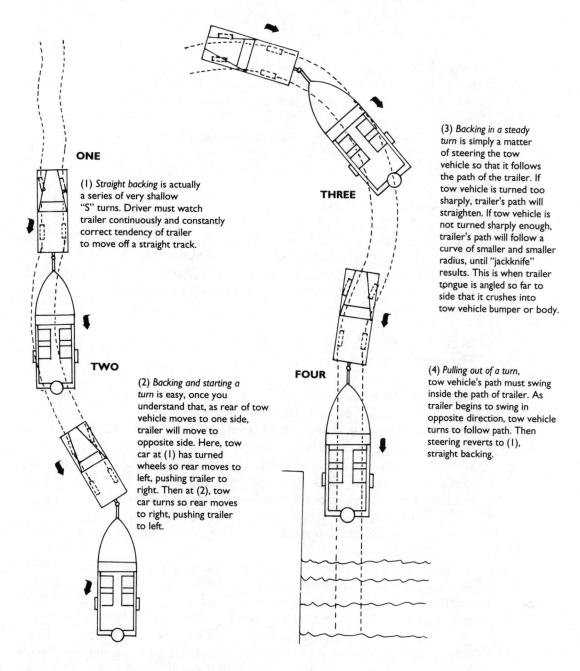

ONE

(1) *Straight backing* is actually a series of very shallow "S" turns. Driver must watch trailer continuously and constantly correct tendency of trailer to move off a straight track.

TWO

(2) *Backing and starting a turn* is easy, once you understand that, as rear of tow vehicle moves to one side, trailer will move to opposite side. Here, tow car at (1) has turned wheels so rear moves to left, pushing trailer to right. Then at (2), tow car turns so rear moves to right, pushing trailer to left.

THREE

(3) *Backing in a steady turn* is simply a matter of steering the tow vehicle so that it follows the path of the trailer. If tow vehicle is turned too sharply, trailer's path will straighten. If tow vehicle is not turned sharply enough, trailer's path will follow a curve of smaller and smaller radius, until "jackknife" results. This is when trailer tongue is angled so far to side that it crushes into tow vehicle bumper or body.

FOUR

(4) *Pulling out of a turn,* tow vehicle's path must swing inside the path of trailer. As trailer begins to swing in opposite direction, tow vehicle turns to follow path. Then steering reverts to (1), straight backing.

Finally, use common sense. With a trailer in tow, you'll want to anticipate your driving moves farther in advance; that in turn means driving slower and much more deliberately than you would without a trailer. For example, you should get used to braking sooner rather than more aggressively. And remember that patience is always a virtue, but especially so when trailering. Above all things, be cautious, drive defensively — as though all the cars around you are being driven by drunken idiots — and be polite. If you drive with extra courtesy and caution, in most instances other drivers will reciprocate.

So . . . you've mastered the art of driving with a trailer in tow, and now you've just pulled off the highway and into the launching ramp area. What do you do next? Simple — just follow these seven easy steps.

Step One: Try to Relax

Remember, you want this to be fun, not a hassle. Take it slow, and be cool. For example, don't immediately dive for a place at the launching ramp. Park your rig *away* from the launching area, to keep clear of the stream of other trailers trying to get in and out. You have work to do before you launch, and there's no point in holding up others while you do it.

Step Two: Anticipate Potential Problems

After you've safely parked away from the madding crowd, make an inspection tour of the ramp and parking area. Is the ramp steep enough so your transom, skeg, or prop won't hit bottom as it moves off the trailer? If the ramp will fit more than one trailer at a time, is there a certain portion that's particularly popular? If so, try to find out why. Is there a lip or ledge at the lower end of the ramp that might make retrieval difficult if the trailer wheels go past it? If the water is tidal, is its depth decreasing, perhaps to the point that the ramp will be bone-dry by the time you're ready to launch? Is the ramp surface slippery with algae and mud, which could reduce tow vehicle traction or send you slip-slidin' away as you walk aft to use the winch?

Is there a dock or float to secure your floating boat after launch, or will someone need to start the engine and circle, anchor, or beach the boat while the empty trailer is towed to a parking space? Is there a strong breeze to be taken into account if the boat is not to be blown offshore or back onto the trailer?

Check out the parking lot. Is a special area set aside for car-trailer combinations, or after launching will the driver have to unhitch the trailer and park it separately? If the latter, be sure the driver has the know-how and strength to do the job without assistance. If your trailer has a tongue jack equipped with a pivoting rubber-tired caster wheel, it'll be a big help here. And if you're launching a sailboat, look for overhead power lines. Aluminum masts and high-tension wires don't mix.

Step Three: Prep the Boat and Trailer for Launch

Walk around your rig, mentally running through the exercise you're about to begin. Here's a checklist of common activities that need doing *before* you get to the ramp:

• If you didn't gas up the boat at an automotive service station before arrival, and there's a station nearby, now's the time to go back and do it. You don't want to run out of fuel in the middle of the lake — and if you use a land-based gas station, you're likely to save a dime a gallon or more on the transaction compared with marina prices.

• If the picnic lunch, the waterskis, the cooler, and the boom box are still in the car, move them to the boat before launching so you don't have to go wading or lug the stuff over long distances later.

• Except for the winch line hooked into the bow eye, release all the tie-downs securing the boat to the trailer.

• Make sure the engine or I/O unit is in "up" position.

• If your taillights and wiring system aren't fully waterproofed (most aren't), disconnect the wiring harness between car and trailer to avoid blown fuses.

• Tighten any loose drain plugs. Otherwise, your cockpit may start to fill with water as soon as the transom is immersed.

• Secure one or two long docking lines to deck cleats and place the coils of line on deck within easy reach of anyone standing at the tongue end of the trailer. With a bow line to shore, the boat will be under control immediately after launching.

• If you're launching singlehandedly and there's no adjacent dock to tie up to right after getting afloat, secure a lunch anchor to the end of one of the docking lines. Then, after launch, you can nudge the boat into shore, jump off the bow onto land, and secure the boat with the anchor while you park the trailer and tow vehicle.

• If you plan on immersing your wheels, you should have already installed bearing protectors, which help keep the grease in and the water out (see Chapter 10 for details on how these clever gadgets work). Check to be sure the pistons in the protectors are pushed to the compressed position (i.e. outward, away from the trailer). If they're not, give them a shot or two from your grease gun.

If you've just arrived after a long, high-speed tow, your wheel bearings may be hot. If so, let them sit for 15 minutes or so to cool. That way they're less likely to be warped or cracked by sudden immersion in cold water.

Step Four: Move the Trailer Down the Ramp

With the fuel tank filled, tie-downs cast off, prop in "up" mode, electrics disconnected, drain plug in place, supplies on board, lines and anchor at the ready and hubs pressurized, you're ready to back down the ramp. If there are others ahead of you, offer assistance; it's not only courteous but may also cut down your waiting time.

When your turn comes to launch, whether you'll have to dunk the trailer hubs depends mostly on the slope of the launching ramp and the type of boat and trailer you have. If you have a fixed-bunk trailer, most likely you'll have to immerse the trailer wheels all the way to the top of the tires in order to get the boat to slide off. On the other hand, if you have a fully rollered trailer properly fitted to the boat, and the ramp you're on is reasonably steep, you may be able to keep the wheel hubs above water and thus avoid the grease-gun routine. Just be sure you roll the trailer down to where the water's deep enough so the boat doesn't hit bottom before she gains full buoyancy and floats away.

In backing down the ramp, take it slow; remember, your tow vehicle isn't waterproof. Don't back down until the tailpipe is practically kissing the water's surface. Leave at least a few inches for safety, and remember the danger of surprise wakes from passing powerboats.

Step Five: Secure the Tow Vehicle on the Ramp

Boat launching ramps come in all degrees of slope. Steep ramps — with slopes in the range of 20 feet of drop per 100 feet horizontally, termed a "20% slope" — may cause a light tow vehicle attached to a relatively heavy boat to begin to skid backward on the ramp, particularly if the surface is wet or slimy. If you foresee that possibility, proceed with extra caution. Reducing air pressure in all four tires by 5 pounds or so (only while on the ramp, of course) may provide the extra traction needed. So may piling a couple of hundred pounds of sandbags in the trunk, throwing sand on the surface of a slimy ramp, or — if you have one of the new front-wheel-drive cars, which often have traction problems on steep ramps — asking a crowd of your heavyweight friends to stand on the front bumper. That, however, is a procedure I definitely *don't* recommend, for safety reasons.

Pulling a loaded trailer *up* a steep, wet ramp is almost always harder than backing *down* the ramp. If you have any doubt that your particular vehicle can do the job, make a test run first. That is, back halfway down the ramp, then try to move forward. If you have trouble doing so, abort the launch and find a ramp with a shallower incline.

Assuming you've overcome all these problems and the trailer is now immersed to the required extent, try to leave someone with the vehicle if possible. If that can't be done, be sure to turn off the engine and use the emergency brake as well as the gearshift to hold the vehicle in place. If you have any doubt that the vehicle will stay put after taking these measures, use wheel chocks as well.

Step Six: Move the Boat off the Trailer

With the winch handle firmly in hand, switch the ratchet to "off" and begin winding out the bow line. If your winch has a brake lever, use it to help control the boat's movement. If the ramp is steep and you have a roller-equipped trailer, the boat should begin moving immediately. If it doesn't, *don't* let go the winch handle and begin pushing. Instead, continue cranking out bow line until you have a couple of feet of slack. Then click in the ratchet *before* you release the winch handle. If you let the handle spin by itself, you might suddenly find yourself in the hospital with a broken wrist, or worse.

Now you — and a helper or two if possible — can push until the boat begins to roll. Of course, given a well-adjusted rig in first-class condition, you shouldn't have to do any pushing; the boat should roll off the trailer like water off a duck's back. But if the rollers are corroded, worn, or improperly spaced under the boat, a push or two may be necessary to get things moving.

An alternative to using gravity or manpower to get the boat moving is to start the engine and back off. That's okay if the engine drive is immersed deeply enough to submerge the prop and cooling water intake, and if there's not so much mud and silt in the area that the engine's cooling system might become fouled. But with a roller-equipped trailer, running the engine to launch shouldn't be necessary.

If your trailer is bunker-equipped, you'll need to go deeper, making it easier to use the engine to drive the boat off. In any case, if you use the engine to power the boat off, let it warm up for a couple of minutes before shifting into gear, or it may stall. While waiting, check cooling water flow, and if you have gauges, check oil pressure.

If your boat rides high on the trailer and you want to use a relatively shallow ramp (say with a slope of 1 in 10 — 10% — or so), you may not be able to back far enough to get the boat afloat without endangering your tow vehicle. Then your only alternative may be to get yourself a trailer tongue extension like the one pictured in Figure 4-6.

Step Seven: Secure Boat, Trailer, and Tow Vehicle Away from the Ramp.

Once your boat is afloat, secure her immediately and move the trailer and tow vehicle off the ramp so the next launcher can start working. Don't dawdle; the next guy in line is probably even more anxious than you are to get going.

That's about all there is to launching. In most cases, it's actually a lot quicker and less complicated than it sounds. It takes practice, but after you've launched 10 or 20 times, you'll probably have the routine down pat and you'll be able to do the whole job in 10 minutes or less.

Retrieving: Launching in Reverse

Retrieving a boat is like launching played backward, with a few minor changes. You simply bring the boat into a nearby dock or to the water's edge, move the trailer into position (no deeper than necessary to get the boat started on center-line), run the boat up onto the trailer, hook onto the winch, grind in, and drive the rig out onto dry land.

If you have a helper, he or she can wait with the winch line while you gently nose the boat as far onto the trailer as you can with the engine. Then he snaps the line into the boat's bow eye and cranks in the initial tension while you hold the boat in position with the engine. Once there's tension on the line, you can cut power.

With rollered trailers not deeply immersed, the boat may move only halfway onto the trailer before the winch must be brought to bear. With more deeply immersed bunk-type trailers, the engine may be able to push the boat all the way up to the vee-chock at the bow, in which case the winch is used only to snug down the boat the last inch or so. (If you run the boat up with the engine, be sure there will be enough water under the prop to avoid hitting bottom, even with the bow raised somewhat. Also, don't use too much throttle or you may pit the prop blades through cavitation.)

If there's a crosswind or crosscurrent at the ramp, guide bars or positioning poles (Figure 3-1) can be helpful. Just gently bump the bow against the inside of the downwind or downstream pole, steer toward the center of the trailer, and move ahead slowly. If the poles are properly positioned, the boat will usually center herself without fuss.

With the boat secured to the trailer at the bow, you're ready to tow up the ramp. Use low gear, and apply the gas gently to avoid spinning your wheels.

The secret of success in launching and retrieving boils down to three main points: (1) The trailer must be suitable both for the boat and for the ramp being used (as explained in Chapters 3 and 7), (2) the tow vehicle must be up to the job (Chapters 5 and 6), and (3) practice makes perfect. With a pastime as pleasant as boating, getting that practice can be half the fun.

PART FOUR

How to Maintain and Repair Your Trailer

CHAPTER TEN.

Checking and Maintaining Tires and Wheels

any boat people pay little or no attention to their trailer's tires and wheels, but that can be a mistake. Here's why.

Tires

If the Load Capacity is too Low, Your Tires may Blow

Make sure the maximum capacity for your tires, stamped on the sidewall, is equal to or greater than the load being carried divided by the number of tires. There's no harm in having tires with an extra-high capacity. If your tires are rated for significantly more load than you're carrying, you can use Figure 10-1 to find the minimum pressure you'll need to support the load properly. By reducing the pressure to the value indicated you can give your boat a softer, more cushioned ride without sacrificing safety or significantly reducing tire life.

Underinflation can Overheat and Blow Your Tires Too

That's why it's a good idea to check the inflation pressure frequently and make sure it's at the proper level, per the sidewall information or per Figure 10-1.

Tread Wear can Kill a Tire

But it's not likely to, since the vast majority of trailer boaters don't accumulate the high mileage needed to wear away a tire tread. Nevertheless it's worth

Figure 10-1

Trailer tire inflation pressure versus capacity

SMALL TIRES

TIRE SIZE DESIGNATION	TIRE LOAD LIMITS (LBS.) AT VARIOUS COLD INFLATION PRESSURES (PSI)																	
	15	20	25	30	35	40	45	50	55	60	65	70	75	80	85	90	95	100
4.80-8	260	310	350	390(A)	430	465	495	530	560	590(B)	615	645	670	695	720	745(C)		
4.80-12	345	410	465	520	570	615	660	700	740	780(B)	815	855	890	920	955	990(C)		
5.30-12	395	465	530	590	645	700	745	795	840(B)	885	925	970	1010	1045(C)				
5.70-8	355	420	480	530	580	630	675	715(B)	760	800	835	875	910(C)	945	980	1010	1045	1075(D)
6.90-9	500	590(A)	670	750	820	885(B)	950	1010	1065	1120(C)	1175	1225	1280	1325	1375(D)	1420	1470	1510(E)
6.50-10	530	625	715	795	870	940	1010	1070	1135	1190(C)	1250	1305	1360	1410	1460	1510	1560	1605(E)
7.50-10	695	820	935	1040	1135	1230	1315	1400	1480	1560	1635	1705	1775	1845	1910	1975(E)		

LARGE TIRES

TIRE SIZE DESIGNATION	TIRE LOAD LIMITS (LBS.) AT VARIOUS COLD INFLATION PRESSURES (PSI)										
	15	20	25	30	35	40	45	50	55	60	65
6.50-13 ST	650	770	875	975	1065(B)	1150	1235	1315(C)			
7.75-15 ST	830	985	1120	1245	1365(B)	1475	1580	1680(C)			
8.55-15 ST	990	1170	1330	1480	1620(B)	1755	1880	2000(C)	2115	2225	2330(D)
"78 SERIES"											
A78-13 ST	600	710	810	900	985(B)	1065	1140	1215(C)			
B78-13 ST	650	770	875	975	1065(B)	1155	1235	1315(C)			
C78-13 ST	695	825	940	1045	1145(B)	1235	1325	1410(C)			
E78-14 ST	790	935	1065	1185	1300(B)	1405	1505	1600(C)			
F78-14 ST	845	1000	1140	1270	1385(B)	1500	1605	1710(C)			
G78-14 ST	920	1090	1245	1385	1515(B)	1635	1755	1865(C)			
H78-14 ST	1005	1190	1355	1510	1650(B)	1785	1910	2035(C)			
E78-15 ST	790	935	1065	1185	1300(B)	1405	1505	1600(C)			
F78-15 ST	845	1000	1140	1270	1385(B)	1500	1605	1710(C)			
G78-15 ST	920	1090	1245	1385	1515(B)	1635	1755	1865(C)			
H78-15 ST	1005	1190	1355	1510	1650(B)	1785	1910	2035(C)	2150	2260	2370(D)
"70 SERIES"											
F70-14 ST	845	1000	1140	1270	1385(B)	1500	1605	1710(C)			
H70-14 ST	1005	1190	1355	1510	1650(B)	1785	1910	2035(C)			

Note: "Load Range" is a measure of tire carcass strength as defined by the "ply rating." That is, Load Rating A is equivalent to a 2-ply rating, B to a 4-ply rating, C to 6-ply, D to 8-ply, and so on up to N, equivalent to a 24-ply rating. (Incidentally, under certain conditions, the actual number of plies may differ from the "ply rating," though this is of no consequence to the trailer-boater.)

Letters in parentheses denote Load Range for which bold-face loads and inflations are maximum. For example, a 5.70-8 tire rated for Load Range B can support a maximum of 715 pounds, for Load Range C 910 pounds, and for Load Range D 1,075 pounds.

Source: Tire and Rim Association

checking occasionally. You can use the "dime test" or check out the tire's built-in wear indicators. That is, current federal safety standards dictate that every new tire must have tread wear indicators spaced around its circumference (four indicators on 8- to 12-inch tires, six on 13- to 15-inch sizes). When you get down to an eighth of an inch of tread, the wear indicator begins to show through, making intermittent rings around the tire's circumference. Then you know it's time to replace the tire.

Old Age is Another Common
Cause of Tire Demise
After 10 to 15 years of occasional use, the tread on your trailer tires may still be fine. But the sun's ultraviolet rays and long-term exposure to the natural ozone in the air may have had a deteriorating effect, and the tire sidewalls might begin to develop small stress cracks and crevices that run circumferentially around the sidewalls. If so, it's time for replacement. Otherwise, the first time the old tire is subjected to a shock load, it may pop.

Using the Wrong Type of Tire
May Cause Towing Problems
Modern trailer tires generally have one of three different constructions (Figure 10-2). *Diagonal bias tires* have fabric reinforcing — either nylon or polyester — with the same number of plies on the sidewalls as on the tread area. *Belted bias tires* have diagonally biased fabric plies plus extra plies in a belt on the tread area. *Radial tires* typically have one ply wrapped around the body of the tire plus two layers — usually of steel wire rather than nylon or polyester — in a belt around the tread area.

Although almost all passenger car tires these days are radials, bias tires for use on boat trailers are still common. In fact, in the smaller sizes (8- to 12-inch wheels), radial tires aren't even available, at least not yet.

However, radial tires in the 13-, 14-, and 15-inch size are now available for boat trailer use and some folks predict that the supply of biased tires in these sizes will gradually become more and more limited.

To some trailer industry folks, that's lamentable. Their reasoning is that the stiffer sidewalls of biased tires seem to help a boat trailer track better compared with "squishy" radial tires, which, they feel, tend to accentuate any tendency to wander from side to side.

Bias-tire advocates also point out that the bulgy sidewalls of radial tires, with but a single ply in the wall, are often more prone to snagging, punctures, and ruptures from uneven terrain, rocks, and underwater obstructions.

The Wrong Spare can
Cause Problems Too
In the old days, if you had the same size tow-vehicle tires and trailer tires, you could interchange them with no problem, thus saving the extra cost and bother of a special spare tire just for the trailer. Now, though, even if your tow-vehicle

Figure 10-2.
Tire types

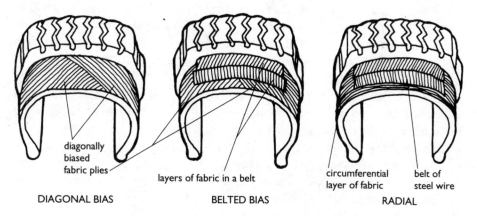

diagonally
biased
fabric plies

layers of fabric in a belt

circumferential
layer of fabric

belt of
steel wire

DIAGONAL BIAS   BELTED BIAS   RADIAL

and trailer tire sizes are the same, the chances are 99 out of 100 that your tow car or truck is equipped with radials. Hence you'll have to decide if you want to take a chance on using radials on your trailer and possibly aggravating sway, or if you should stick with bias-type trailer tires and dedicate a spare exclusively to the trailer.

If you decide to go with radials on your trailer, you should know that tire-industry standard load limits for passenger tires used for trailer service are to be reduced by a factor of 1.1. That's mainly because trailer tires — which are marked with the suffix "ST" (for "special trailer") — are generally designed with more muscle, durability, and resistance to bruises and impact breaks in their sidewalls.

If you have a tandem trailer, you might be tempted to mix radials and bias tires in pairs. I wouldn't, for two reasons. First, the differences in resistance to sway may put undue strain on the sidewalls of the bias pair. And second, even when the tires are supposedly of the same size, small differences in what is called in tire circles "the loaded radius" — the distance from the center of the hub down to the ground — may shift too much of the total load onto the tires with the larger loaded radius.

Rims, Bolts, and Studs

Rusty or dented rims, against which the tire bead can't get a good "seat," are a frequent cause of blowouts. Even brand-new trailer rims are often poorly protected from rust and start to corrode right after the first ramp dunking. To help prevent premature rusting, wire-brush and coat each rim (even new ones) right up to the tire bead with a good antirust paint. If rim dents might interfere with proper tire seating, replace the rim.

When replacing old rims, be careful to get exactly the same configuration as the original. Try to take the old rim along and *carefully* match it against the new, in the store. A tire dealer once tried to sell me a rim that was identical except that its center hole was about an eighth of an inch bigger than the hub diameter, whereas the original rim was a close sliding fit over the hub. The dealer claimed that the rim hole size didn't make any difference, but it was obvious to me that the close-fitting hub was designed to help ease some of the load on the four lug bolts that held the rim in place. When I resisted buying, he said that my old rim was obsolete and the only size currently made was the size he was offering. He was wrong on that score, too, as I found out by checking other dealers. If you have trouble finding a dealer who is willing and able to order the exact rim you need, try contacting Design Wheel & Hub in Akron, Ohio. Their address and phone number are in Appendix 3.

Another thing to be sure to match is the diameter and type of bolt circle (or stud circle if your hub has studs instead of bolts). Some circles have four bolts or studs, others have five, and a few have six. Know the diameter and type you need before visiting your dealer.

A couple of other caveats. First, before every trip, check to be sure no lug bolts or studs are missing and that each one is wrench-tight. I'm always surprised when visiting launching ramps by how many trailer wheels I see with missing bolts or studs. Second, when reinstalling a wheel, hand-tighten all lug bolts or nuts first, and then, proceeding in a clockwise direction, tighten each bolt or nut a few fractions of a turn at a time with a wrench, using the wheel torquing chart in Figure 10-3 as a guide, until all are tight.

Wheel Bearings

As explained in Chapter 9, if you plan on immersing your wheels, you should install bearing protectors (Figure 10-4), which help keep the grease in and the water out.

The reason for this is simple. When the hubs hit the water they'll be suddenly cooled, and the grease and trapped air inside the hubs will rapidly shrink. Without the spring-driven pistons moving inward to keep the smaller volume under pressure, sudden cooling can draw water into the hubs and onto the bearing surfaces. You'll want to avoid that situation if at all possible, since water plus steel roller bearings equals rust. Without bearing protectors, you'd need to dismantle and repack your wheel bearings every time you launched — a messy, unpleasant job (described in Chapter 12), and an expensive one if you farm it out.

Figure 10-3. *Wheel torquing chart* *(for standard trailer* *wheels)*	Stud Size (diameter)	Foot-Pounds of Torque
	½"	70 to 90
	9/16"	110 to 140
	5/8"	125 to 140

Figure 10-4.

Wesbar Auto-Lube bearing protector

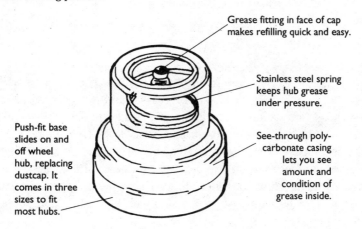

Grease fitting in face of cap
makes refilling quick and easy.

Stainless steel spring
keeps hub grease
under pressure.

Push-fit base
slides on and
off wheel
hub, replacing
dustcap. It
comes in three
sizes to fit
most hubs.

See-through poly-
carbonate casing
lets you see
amount and
condition of
grease inside.

Consequently, carry in your tow vehicle a small cartridge-type grease gun filled with a 14-ounce cartridge of premium-quality grease, and as explained in Chapter 9, pump out the piston on each hub just before launching.

Incidentally, it's smart to keep some sort of cover over the grease fitting on the hub; otherwise dirt and grime will stick to the loose grease, and you'll have to wipe the gunk away every time you grease up. You can buy a close-fitting plastic cover made for the purpose — or in a pinch, you can pull a sandwich Baggie over each hub and hold it in place with a couple of rubber bands. This looks a bit weird but works fine.

CHAPTER ELEVEN.
Other Routine Maintenance

A side from checking tires and keeping wheel bearings clean, full of grease, and properly adjusted, only a few other chores are needed to maintain your trailer in first-class condition. Mainly it's a matter of checking out the trailer periodically to make sure that corrosion, chafe, or unusual stresses and strains haven't created problems that might need correction, and of judicious application of a little oil or grease here and there. The following are hints on where to look for potential problems and what to do about them, along with some suggestions on lubrication and other simple periodic maintenance tasks.

Dealing with Rust

Technically, rust is the product of chemical oxidation of iron, in the presence of oxygen, to a reddish, brittle, porous material consisting mostly of ferrous or iron oxide. It occurs when steel (an alloy of iron, carbon, and other minor elements) comes in contact with water for an extended period. If salt is present in the water, oxidation progresses faster. On a boat trailer, it eats away at all exposed surfaces of steel, causing gradual thinning of the base material, and eventually complete disintegration. There are various ways to slow down or eliminate rusting. Here are seven:

1. If possible, keep the trailer away from water, and especially salt water. If a boat hoist rather than a launching ramp is used to launch and retrieve the boat from her trailer, water will have a harder time infiltrating cracks, crevices, and tubes.

2.   Rinse salt water off the trailer as soon as possible after using a launching ramp. Some boating magazine writers advise readers to "rinse off immediately after immersion at the ramp," but for many of us this is not a practical alternative. I've visited dozens of public launching ramps up and down the U.S. East Coast and have yet to see one with running fresh water and a hose for rinsing. Maybe all the rampside spigots are in California. Anyway, don't count on being able to use an immediate rinse as a remedy for corrosion. But rinsing with fresh water as soon as possible — even the next day if need be — can still have some beneficial effect.

If the trailer has drum brakes and you launch in salt water, consider installing a brake flush kit to rinse internal brake parts. Such a kit (available from International Trailer Parts, among others) pipes water inside the drum mechanism so a jet of water is aimed right at the source of potential problems. Even better is to switch to disk brakes, which are right out in the open where you can hit them with a garden hose.

3.   Dig out and clean off any built-up or dried-on mud, road dirt, and dust. These absorb moisture, thus promoting corrosion. Check especially in the front ends of any open-tube frame components, where road dirt and debris can be pushed in by the slipstream as you barrel down the highway.

4.   Coat all moving parts with oil or grease. Oil, which I recommend for use on accessories such as winches or dolly wheel caster mechanisms, will wash off in the weather. Therefore you'll need to oil such parts every month or two during the season to keep them in first-class operating condition. If you've ignored them for too long, they may not respond to a mere squirt of oil. Then try WD-40 or CRC spray, or a good penetrating oil. Work it in by operating the mechanism, and when it seems to spin or move smoothly again, follow with a good dose of lubricating oil. Regular crankcase oil (10W-40 or straight 30-grade, for example) works fine, dispensed from a push-bottom oilcan available in practically any hardware store.

5.   Try rustproofing with chemicals. Several materials are on the market, such as Duro Auto Rustproofing Exterior Formula AR-3, an aerosol spray distributed by Loctite Corporation Automotive and Consumer Group, Cleveland, Ohio. Duro claims its stuff will "protect against damaging rust and corrosion. Provides a tough, abrasion-resistant coating against the harmful effects of water, salt, road tar, ashes, gasoline, and other road chemicals." Or you can ask any of a number of automotive rustproofing companies, such as Ziebart, to spray their version of petroleum-based gunk inside the tube frame and all the hidden corners of your rig. Most of these materials dry to a waxy, sticky, greasy finish, so treat only surfaces such as the interior of frame tubes that won't be rubbed against in the normal course of things.

6. Use rust-preventive paint. I've tried Rustoleum with success. Be sure to get the type specially formulated to inhibit rust on steel. After wiping away any loose rust particles, grease, and road dirt and wire-brushing the clean surface, you can paint Rustoleum right over any remaining rust. It seems to penetrate the cracks and crevices well. Pettit makes a similar product called TrailerCoat.

7. Avoid using a painted steel trailer. That is, buy a galvanized or an aluminum trailer if you can afford the extra cost. Note, however, that even galvanized and aluminum trailers generally use steel axles, bearings, wheel hubs, wheels, couplers, and taillight components (although some of these components may also be galvanized) — so while the rust problem may be lessened by going to a "non-steel" trailer, it isn't eliminated.

Keeping Up the Finish

If your trailer is painted but is new, well primed, and sprayed with extra coats of glossy enamel, it may be worth polishing and waxing the surface once or twice a year to help keep out moisture, and it'll make the trailer gleam with a concours elegance. But all the brackets, joints, and multiple structural members on most trailers make the job difficult. Furthermore, if and when rust shows up and you want to repaint, you'll have to clean the whole thing off with a wax-removing chemical — not an easy job. So if you've just acquired a used trailer or a new but plainly painted one and you don't care about pinstriping or color coordination with your tow vehicle, you may prefer to start by overcoating with a rust-inhibiting paint. It won't be fancy, but it'll look neat and workmanlike and will definitely help prevent corrosion.

Checking Structural Soundness

This usually is not difficult, especially if the boat is off the trailer. Look for rails and other frame components that are bent or asymmetrical with components on the opposite side. Wiggle everything and test the tightness of all nuts and bolts with a wrench. Where bends or joints occur, check for cracks or breaks in the metal. Pay particular attention to welds, where crevice corrosion can weaken a joint to the point of failure. When in doubt, give the questionable area a good whack with the trusty three-pound sledge hammer from your toolkit, and see if anything gives or if the noise it produces is more of a dull "thunk" than a sonorous "ping" or "clang." If so, you might want to have a welder beef up the area with a steel patch. Any journeyman welder can do the job.

Checking the Ball and Coupler

Inspect the hitch ball for cracks and worn or flat spots. Be sure it's wrench-tight on its platform, snug against its lockwasher. If there's no lockwasher under the platform, install one immediately.

Check the coupler for rust, strain distortions, cracks, and proper adjustment of the clamp. The clamp should bear against the ball fairly tightly — so that there is practically no play in the system — but not tightly enough to bind when the tow vehicle turns. If it's too tight or too loose, you can adjust it by turning the handwheel or, in the case of a lever-type closure, the nut underneath (Figure 11-1). To keep the mechanism in first-class condition, place a few drops of oil on the threads of the handwheel or the pivot points in the latching mechanism and spray in an occasional shot of WD-40 or CRC from the bottomside up.

Figure 11-1.
Coupler clamps

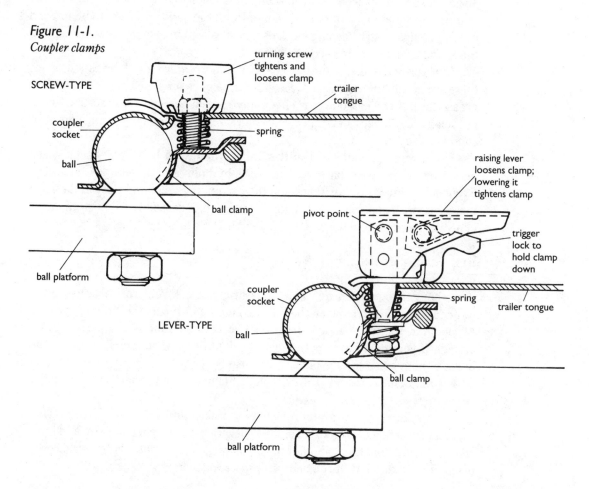

Checking the Suspension

Many leaf springs need to be lubricated in two places: at the end pivot points (unless the bushings are rubber rather than steel, in which case they need no lubrication but if dried out and cracked will need replacement), and between the leaves. When installed, the springs probably got a coating of thick grease both on the pivots and between the leaves, which will last for a long time — probably several years. But it's a good idea eventually to force in some new grease if you can.

Sometimes the end hangers or bushings have grease fittings installed, and then it's just a matter of a few pumps with your grease gun. But forcing grease between leaves of a spring is almost impossible without taking the spring apart, and that's not usually worth the time and effort. If the spring looks weak or worn, or you suspect a cracked leaf, replacement is almost always easier and cheaper in the long run than an attempted repair. But if the spring appears to be in good condition, you can try keeping its sides smeared with grease rather than painting them, and chances are it'll stay that way.

Coil springs and torsion bars usually don't require any lubrication, since there are no rubbing metal surfaces. The same goes for shock absorbers, unless grease fittings are evident. But check any rubber bushing for cracks or wear; eventually they'll need to be replaced. Check with your trailer's manufacturer for sources of supply.

Leaf springs are attached to the trailer frame with hangers, shackles, and equalizer or stabilizer bars held in place by bolts and sometimes bushings. Eventually these bolts, bushings, and their mounting holes will wear to the point that some or all of the assembly must be replaced. A careful visual inspection will generally be enough to reveal what, if anything, needs to be done.

Inspecting Brakes and Actuators

If you bought your trailer new and it has surge brakes, you probably received an owner's manual that explains how to maintain and repair the braking system. Atwood, for example, has a 16-page booklet devoted entirely to its surge-brake system. If you don't have such a manual, determine what company made your brake system and send for one. (It's probably stamped with the name Atwood, Dico, Null, Bendix, Dexter, Hayes, Toledo Stamping, or Vannor; see Appendix 3 for addresses.)

That said, we won't go into details on brakes and actuators, except (1) to explain how to adjust your brakes, (2) to describe how to check brake fluid level, and (3) to note that lubrication of the actuator (in accordance with your owner's manual) will extend its life and ensure proper functioning.

Adjusting Your Brakes

Your brakes were probably adjusted when new, but after the first thousand miles of towing, and every 2,000 miles thereafter — plus whenever wheel bearings are repacked — they should be adjusted again. The procedure is relatively simple. First, you'll need to raise the wheel you want to adjust off the ground. Then, referring to Figure 11-2, remove the dust clip or cap from the adjusting slot (located at the lower part of the back side of the brake assembly). Insert a brake adjusting tool (made for the purpose and available from most trailer supply stores if one didn't come with your trailer) and rotate the adjustment cog until you can't spin the wheel anymore. At this point, the pair of brake shoes inside the drum is tightened as far as it will go. Now back off on the shoes by reversing the rotation of the adjustment cog — 10 notches for a single-axle trailer or five notches for a dual-axle job. Withdraw the adjusting tool, replace the clip or cap, and move on to the next wheel.

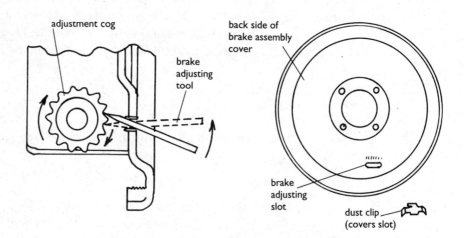

Figure 11-2.
Brake adjustment

adjustment cog

brake
adjusting
tool

back side of
brake assembly
cover

brake
adjusting
slot

dust clip
(covers slot)

Checking Brake Fluid

This is simple; just remove the cap on top of the actuator housing, and if fluid is below about ½ inch from the top, add fluid as per the owner's manual, which usually specifies DOT 3 automotive brake fluid.

Maintaining Lighting Systems

If you have a problem with your lights or don't know how to hook them up to your tow vehicle, see Chapter 12. But if they work fine (so far) and you want to know how to keep them working, read on.

The biggest enemy of good electrical flow is oxidation of contact points, which occurs mainly in moist air. If you smear a little Vaseline or light grease on all plug prongs and receptacles, light bulb sockets, wire splices, and ground connections to the trailer, it'll be a barrier against air and moisture, retard oxidation, and keep your lights running longer.

For additional protection, melt solder around all wire-to-wire splices and then wrap them tightly with plastic electrical tape.

Added insurance for the car-to-trailer connecting plug can be provided by a brief ritual just before each use. First scrape the prongs clean with a penknife or sandpaper and try to scrape off any surface deposits on the receptacle holes with an icepick, rat-tail file, or small piece of sandpaper rolled up around a matchstick. Then, after daubing a little grease on the prongs, push the mating plugs forcefully together as far as they will go and wrap electrical tape around the joint to keep out rain and road spray.

Between uses, keep both halves of the plug protected from weather and scuffing. Frequently you can tuck the plug on the tow vehicle up under the lip of the rear bumper. To ward off dirt, try using a plastic sandwich bag. Slip a Baggie over the top of each half, milk as much air out as possible, twist the open end of the bag into a narrow neck, and slip a rubber band around the neck to hold it in place.

Winter Layup

If you store your boat on a trailer during the off season, you may find these tips helpful:

- Block up the trailer frame a few inches to take its weight off the tires and springs. This will also make it convenient to check wheel bearings, inspect tire tread, remove and paint wheels, etc. Four or five standard cinder blocks, stood on end and capped with 2 x 4 scraps, make good trailer supports.
- Keep water and ice out, preferably using a cover, properly supported to prevent pockets of rainwater or snow. Open the cockpit scuppers, remove drain plugs, and raise the trailer tongue so water drains out.
- Ease tie-downs to help eliminate hull strains and distortions during the layup period.
- Make periodic inspection tours to be sure all is well. The most common off-season storage problem stems from high winds damaging the cover, letting rain in and possibly damaging the boat — particularly if the owner forgot to pull the drain plugs.

That's about all there is to routine preventive maintenance. In the next chapter we'll cover repairs and replacements — which are more likely to be needed if the simple preventive maintenance steps outlined here are ignored or postponed too long.

CHAPTER TWELVE.

Common Repairs and Replacements

Y ou can make most repairs and replacements on your trailer without professional assistance. Given the time and the inclination, you can even order and install a new frame if the old one rusts out. Most of us, however, prefer to deal with more modest repair/replacement projects, of which the two described in this chapter are by far the most common. Read on, and learn how to renew a wheel bearing and how to troubleshoot and repair trailer lights.

How to Renew a Wheel Bearing

Conventional wisdom calls for repacking boat trailer wheels with grease at least once a year, and more often if hubs are frequently immersed in salt water. As part of this repacking process, you can inspect bearings, grease seals, and axles, and replace anything that needs replacing. For a view of what you're getting into, see Figure 12-1. There are a dozen steps in the repacking procedure, as described below.

1. Jack up the Wheel
Working on a level surface and preferably with no boat on the trailer, raise one trailer wheel off the ground by putting a jack under the axle. Before jacking, chock the wheel or wheels on the other side to prevent rolling. On empty tandem trailers, you may be able to elevate one set of wheels without the use of a jack simply by depressing the tongue as low as it will go to raise the back axle, or raising it as high as possible to elevate the front axle.

Figure 12-1.
Wheel hub and bearings

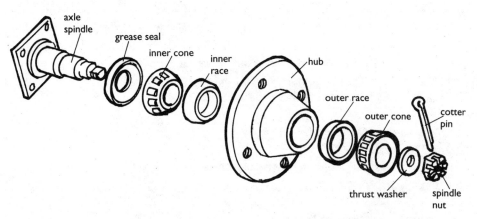

Many axles are hollow tubes, which after a time begin rusting, sometimes from the inside out, thus weakening the skin. Therefore, if you use a jack with a small cross-sectional area at the end of its ram, place a pad such as a short length of 2 x 4 between axle and jack to help prevent crushing the axle surface.

2. Clean Up the Work Site
and Prepare the Hub

Wipe the tire, wheel, and hub clean of road dust, dried mud, and grease at both front side and back. That way there's less chance of dirt getting into the hub innards during the regreasing process.

You can either remove the tire and rim from the hub or leave them in place. Removing them gives you a little more space to work in, but if the hub resists being pulled off, being able to grab the edges of the tire will give you extra leverage.

After cleaning up the area and removing the tire and rim if you choose to do so, spread clean newspapers on the ground below the hub, so that if the hub or bearings inadvertently fall to the ground during disassembly, they won't pick up new dust or dirt. The newspaper also gives you a clean place to lay out your toolkit.

3. Remove the Bearing
Protector or Dustcover

If you haven't already discarded your old dustcovers and installed a set of bearing protectors, I strongly recommend that you switch to them now. The protector (or dustcover) is a press fit into the hub. The easiest way to get it off is to hold a piece of softwood (such as a 2 x 4) against the protector's top outer edge and tap gently with a hammer, spinning the wheel and working gradually around the perimeter of the hub. This will inch the protector outboard, and eventually it'll be loose enough to pull off by hand. Alternatively you can wedge a broad-bladed screwdriver between the hub and inboard edge of the protector and pry it off by twisting the screwdriver blade and working gradually around the perimeter. If it's not pushed on too tightly, you might also be able to wiggle it off using a pair of channel-lock pliers clamped along its axis.

4. Remove the Cotter Pin
and Spindle Nut
Wipe the grease off and inspect the pieces. See if the cotter pin is beginning to get mangled; if so, replace it.

5. Remove the Thrust Washer,
Outer Bearing Cone, and Hub
To do this, grasp the tire (or edge of the hub if you've removed the tire and wheel) on both sides, tilt the top slightly toward you, and jerk outward. That'll dislodge the thrust washer and outer bearing cone, which you can then lift out, clean up, and set aside. Usually the inner cone and seal will then slide off. If they don't, try jerking a second time. If you still have no luck, try tapping the hub assembly off from the back side — but be sure not to dent or score the seal, which is made from thin, pressed steel. If the hub still doesn't come, you may need a wheel puller. Before using one, remove the tire and rim from the hub if you haven't already done so, so the wheel puller can get a grip on the outer edge of the hub. If you don't have a wheel puller and the hub just won't slide off, it may be time to reinstall the wheel and let your local mechanic handle the rest of the job.

Assuming you successfully remove the hub, array the parts on newspaper, being careful not to mix up either the outboard bearing cone or the race with its inboard counterpart.

6. Remove the Grease Seal and
Inboard Cone from the Hub
The best way to do this is to place the hub or rim flat on two parallel blocks of wood, with the seal and cone at the bottom and clean newspapers spread out underneath. After wiping away the grease in the hole in the hub, shove a piece of wood (such as a hammer handle) into the hole, set its end on the face of the inner cone, and tap gently around the perimeter until the grease seal and cone pop out onto the newspapers.

7. Clean Off the Grease
and Examine All Parts

After wiping away the main body of grease with paper towels, you can use kerosene, diesel fuel, or most commercial solvents to dissolve whatever grease remains on any of the pieces you've removed. Avoid gasoline or other highly flammable materials. Wipe all parts clean with paper towels. After cleaning the bearings, spin the rollers in the cones to see if they are free-turning. Examine all parts for rust, pitting, scoring, heat discoloration, or other signs that they need replacing. Check the grease seal for rust and to be sure it's not pitted, scored, bent, or dented, and that rubber parts aren't torn, frayed, or old and embrittled. A good rule is to replace the seals automatically whenever repacking the hubs, to lessen the chance of grease leaking out onto the axle (and water leaking in) through an imperfect seal.

If the axle spindle itself is pitted, badly worn, or scored, it may be a sign that a bearing has frozen and the inner race has been rotating on the spindle rather than on its rollers. You can carefully file off any slight bumps on the spindle, using emery cloth to finish the job.

If the seal surface on the rear of the spindle is roughened by rust, scoring, or pitting (resulting in a poor mating surface with the seal), you can usually repair it with a Bearing Buddy Spindo Seal Kit, available from Unique Functional Products (see Appendix 3 for address). The kit includes a stainless steel collar that fits over the damaged spindle, plus a special O-ring and replacement seal sized to the changed diameter of the spindle.

8. If a Bearing Needs
Replacement, Remove the
Race from the Inside of the Hub

Even if only one of the two bearings appears to need changing, consider replacing both; otherwise, the second one is bound to wear out soon. Be sure to buy exact duplicates. A size designation is usually engraved on the side of the bearing rim to help you match new with old. Also, know that bearings are always replaced as a unit, i.e. the race and the mating bearing cone. Never attempt to "mix and match" parts from different bearings.

To remove a race (which is a press fit in the hub), tap it out using the same wood hammer-handle technique as for the grease seal.

9. Repack the Bearings with
Grease and Begin Reassembly

Reinstall both inner and outer races, if removed, by tapping them back into place. Then clean your hands to make sure you don't contaminate the new grease with dust and grime. Hold a gob of premium-quality wheel bearing grease in the palm of your hand, drop the inner bearing cone into it, and knead the grease until it permeates the insides of the cage (the space between rollers). If you don't want to handle messy grease directly, fill a plastic Baggie with grease, drop the cone in, and knead from the outside. When the inner cone is saturated, set it in its race.

Then tap the grease seal gently into the inner side of the hub using a soft-wood block or rubber hammer to obtain even pressure around the seal's perimeter. Fill the hub with enough new grease to prevent massive air pockets when the hub is installed. Then slip the hub over the spindle.

10. Finish Reassembly

Install a grease-packed outer bearing cone, the thrust washer, and the castle nut (or drilled nut, or hex nut with a keeper) that fits over the end of the threaded spindle. Then begin the bearing adjustment process.

When the nut is hand-tight, spin the wheel and tighten the nut some more until the hub just begins to bind as it turns. Now grab the two sides of the tire or hub and wiggle and push to be sure the hub is firmly seated. Again spin the wheel, and tighten the nut once more until the hub just starts to bind. When you're sure the nut (and nothing else, such as the tire dragging slightly on the ground) is causing the hub to bind slightly, back off one notch (or one hole or one flat) on the nut. The wheel and hub should now spin easily and smoothly; if the hub still binds a little, back off another notch (or hole, or flat). Shake and wiggle the wheel again to be sure there is practically no play. When you're fully satisfied that the bearing is adjusted for smooth operation but doesn't have excess play, put the cotter pin or keeper in place.

Daub the bearing protector almost full with new grease, and smear the mating surfaces with more grease so the protector will slide in easier. Even smeared with grease, it should be a tight fit if it's the right size for the hub. Tap it carefully into place using a wood block to protect it from damage. Check to be sure it's fully seated.

If you're installing a cap rather than a bearing protector as recommended, leave some air space for expansion rather than filling the cap with grease.

Pump the protector with a grease gun until the piston moves off its seat almost but not quite to the top. At that point, stop adding grease, so that the piston can push out a little more when the hub heats up during travel and the grease inside expands.

11. Lower the Wheel to the Ground and Remove the Jack and Chocks

This process is the reverse of Step 1.

12. Clean Up

Wipe off any excess grease from the hub or bearing protector; install a grease cover such as the plastic covers sold for the purpose or a sandwich Baggie as previously described. Wipe off your tools, and go boating!

How to Troubleshoot and Repair Trailer Lights

Water and electricity don't mix. Hence, mostly as a result of their occasional immersion in water, boat trailer lights, wires, and plugs sooner or later tend to malfunction. The end result is always the same: the lights flicker or go out. But the causes vary. Here are some common electrical problems and their solutions.

Individual Light Bulbs Burn out Frequently

That's often because the glass bulbs are hot from use during the trip to the launching ramp, and when they hit the cold water at the ramp, they crack or break. Even "submersible" lights generally aren't waterproof, and may let enough water in to kill bulbs.

There are three good solutions to this problem. First, you can buy a truly waterproof light set. As of this writing, Wesbar's encapsulated unit is the only one I'm aware of that's fully waterproof. Second, you might build a trailer "light bar," which can be mounted on top of your boat during travel and removed before launching. Third, you could put your lights on high guide bars or "stalks" to keep them high and dry. A fourth approach won't solve the problem but may help to lengthen the time between burnouts; that's to disconnect your light plug upon arrival, then wait a half hour or so until the trailer bulbs have cooled off. If none of these solutions appeals to you, you can always carry a bunch of spares and continue to replace the bulbs at frequent intervals.

Light Sockets Corrode, Causing Lights to Operate Intermittently, or Flicker, or Go Out

Any of the solutions for bulb burnouts is likely to help here too. Another fix is a regular program of cleaning the corrosion off the contacts in the socket and then smearing the contacts on both socket and bulb with a little grease or petroleum jelly. To determine whether the socket is the problem, use a voltmeter/ohmmeter, available at Radio Shack for less than $10 the last time I looked. Simply remove the lens and bulb from the suspected socket, connect the trailer wiring to the tow vehicle, turn the trailer lights on, switch the meter to "50 VDC" (volts), and press the prods against the two contact points inside the socket. If you get a steady voltage reading even when you wiggle the prods around a bit, the socket is probably not the problem; try changing bulbs to a known good one. If you get an intermittent voltage reading, the socket probably is the problem. Try cleaning up the contacts or replace the socket. If you get no reading at all, try wiggling the wires behind the socket; maybe there's a loose connection back there.

An Open Circuit Develops, Causing Lights to Go Out

This could be from a broken terminal point, such as at a light fixture, trailer-to-tow-vehicle plug, or ground connection point, or it could be from a broken wire. The first place to look is at all ground terminals; poor ground connections are the most common source of boat trailer electrical difficulties. Do not rely on the coupler connection with the tow vehicle ball to make a good circuit to ground; it won't. Instead, carry a ground wire through the plug from the tow vehicle, and extend it all the way back to the taillights, clipping it right into the lighting circuit as well as the trailer's steel frame. Then you won't have to worry about whether the steel frame is doing its job as a conductor, since the wire is also doing the same job, and better.

If terminal points are not the source of your problem you'll have to search along the connecting wires looking for faults. Since wire insulation can sometimes remain intact even when the conductor inside is broken, it can be difficult to pinpoint the site of an open-circuit problem. But if you inspect every inch of wire carefully, you'll eventually rout out the fault.

Wiring Develops a Short Circuit

The chief source of boat trailer short circuits is chafed wires pinching against the trailer frame or against each other, and eventually wearing through their insulation. To establish that there is a short circuit in the first place, use the volt/ohmmeter switched to "ohms," a measure of electrical resistance. Note that when the two prods touch each other, the needle swings all the way over the scale to zero ohms (i.e. no resistance), indicating there's a short circuit between the prods. If the needle doesn't move at all (i.e. shows an infinite resistance) when you place the prods on two contact points on a wire, it means there's an open circuit between the two points.

With the trailer power plug disconnected, place one prod on "ground" and the other on each of the three plug prongs in turn. The meter should show a high (but not infinitely high) resistance, since the high-resistance light bulb filaments are part of the circuit. If the resistance between prongs is close to zero, there's a short in the circuit.

Turn Signals Blink Too Fast, and/or Flasher Unit in Tow Vehicle Burns Out Frequently

You need a heavy-duty flasher for your vehicle. They're available in most autoparts stores.

The Plug Already Installed on the Trailer Won't Mate with the Plug Already Installed on the Tow Vehicle

You can replace one or the other plug with one that does mate, or buy an adapter plug that mates with both halves. Westbar, for instance, sells two versions of a "round-to-flat" four-pin adapter.

If you're replacing a plug, be careful to match the colors of the wires, which have been standardized for boat trailer use. See Figure 7-2 for information on which color is supposed to go where. If you're hooking up lights on a new trailer or tow vehicle, the diagram and accompanying notes should give you all you need to know to do the job.

Tow Vehicle has Turn-signal Light Circuit Separate from Brake-light Circuit (e.g. amber blinkers but red brake lights)

You'll need to buy a taillight "black box" converter, available from Cole-Hersee, Shelby Industries, Wesbar, and a number of other suppliers.

The Turn-signal Lights on the Tow Vehicle Don't Flash Simultaneously with the Trailer Lights

Try reversing the yellow and green leads at the connector plug. Make sure that the brown leads from each side of the plug are mated, and that the white ground wire is solidly grounded on both sides of the plug.

After a Short Circuit is Found and Fixed, Neither Trailer nor Tow Vehicle Lights Work

Check the lighting fuse in the tow vehicle. (See your vehicle Owner's Manual for location.) It's probably burned out.

The End of our Story . . . but Just for Now

When I started this writing project, I thought it would be little more than a booklet. But now I find that even this book offers barely enough room to cram in all the information. And more new stuff — accessories, trailer designs, ways of doing things — is constantly coming to my attention.

In a couple of years, I'll probably revise and update *Boat Trailers and Tow Vehicles*. Meanwhile, if you note something I haven't covered that you think would interest readers, please write me (in care of the publisher) and let me know. Maybe I'll include it in the next edition.

Trailer Towing Regulations by State

State	Maximum Length With Trailer(s)	Of Trailer and Load			Min. Wt. Requiring Trailer Brakes (lbs.)	Safety Chains	Stop Lights and Turn Signals	Taillights	Clearance Lights	License Light	Reflectors	Flares	Breakaway Brakes	Tiedowns	Insurance
		Length	Width	Height											
Alabama	60'	N/S	8'	13'6"	N/S		X	X	X	X	X	X		N/S	N/S
Alaska	70'	40'	8'6"	14'	N/S	X	X	X	X	X	X				Yes
Arizona		N/S	8'	13'6"	3000	X	X	X	X	X	X	X	X	X	Yes
Arkansas	65'	N/S	8'6"	13'6"	N/S	X	X	X	X	X	X				Yes
California	65'	40'	8'6"	14'	3000	X	X	X	X	X	X	X²	X³	X	Yes
Colorado	70'	40'	8'6"	13'	6000	X	X	X	X	X	X	X	X	X	Yes
Connecticut	60'	48'	8'6"	13'6"	3000	X	X	X	X	X				X	Yes
Delaware	60'	53'	8'6"	13'6"	4001	X	X	X	X	X	X			N/S	Yes
Florida	60'	N/S	8'6"	13'6"	N/S	X	X	X	X	X			X	X	Yes
Georgia	65'	53'	8'6"	13'6"	N/S	X	X	X	X	X	X	X	X	N/S	N/S
Hawaii	60'	40'	9'	13'6"	3000	X	X	X	X	X			X⁴	N/S	No
Idaho	75'	48'	8'6"	14'	1500		X	X	X	X	X	X	X		Yes
Illinois	60'	42'	8'	13'6"	3000	X	X	X	X	X	X	X	X⁵	X	Yes
Indiana	60'	N/S	8'6"	13'6"	3000	X	X	X	X	X	X		X	X	Yes
Iowa	60'	53'	8'6"	13'6"	3000	X	X	X	X	X			X⁴	X	No
Kansas	65'	N/S	8'6"	13'6"		X	X	X	X⁶	X	X	X		X	Yes
Kentucky	55'	N/S	8'	13'6"	N/S	X	X	X	X	X	X			N/S	No
Louisiana	N/S	30'	8'6"	13'6"	3000	X	X	X	X	X	X		X	X	Yes
Maine	65'	48'	8'6"	13'6"	3000	X	X	X	X	X	X	X		X	Yes
Maryland	55'	55'	8'	13'6"	3000	X	X	X	X	X	X		X	X	Yes
Massachusetts	60'	N/S	8'6"	13'6"	10,000	X	X	X	X	X	X	X			Yes
Michigan	55'	N/S	8'6"	13'6"	N/S	X	X	X	X	X	X			N/S	N/S
Minnesota	65'	45'⁷	8'6"	13'6"	1500	X	X	X	X	X	X	X	X⁸	X	Yes
Mississippi	60'	50'	8'6"	13'6"	2000	X	X	X	X	X	X	X	X	N/S	N/S
Missouri	65'	N/S	8'6"	14'	N/S		X	X		X	X			X	Yes⁹
Montana	65'	N/S	8'6"	14'	3000	X	X	X	X	X	X		X⁴		Yes
Nebraska	65'	40'	8'6"	14'6"	N/S	X	X	X		X	X		X	X	Yes
Nevada	70'	N/S	8'6"	14'	3000		X	X	X	X	X				Yes

State	Maximum Length With Trailer(s)	Of Trailer and Load			Min. Wt. Requiring Trailer Brakes (lbs.)	Safety Chains	Stop Lights and Turn Signals	Taillights	Clearance Lights	License Light	Reflectors	Flares	Breakaway Brakes	Tiedowns	Insurance
		Length	Width	Height											
New Hampshire	N/S	48'	8'6"	13'6"	3000	X		X	X[6]	X	X				N/S
New Jersey	45'	35'	8'	13'6"	3000	X	X	X		X	X			X	No
New Mexico	65'	40'	8'6"	13'6"	N/S	X	X	X	X	X	X	X	X	X	Yes
New York	60'	45'	8'	13'6"	500	X	X	X	X	X	X	X		X	N/S
North Carolina	60'	45'	8'	13'6"	4000		X	X	X	X	X				No
North Dakota	75'	53'	8'6"	13'6"	3000	X	X	X	X	X	X			X	No
Ohio	65'	40'	8'6"	13'6"	2000	X	X	X	X	X	X		X	N/S	N/S
Oklahoma	70'	59'6"	8'6"	13'6"	3000	X	X	X	X	X	X		X	X	N/S
Oregon	50'	35'	8'6"	14'	3000	X	X	X	X	X	X			X	No
Pennsylvania	65'	53'	8'6"	13'6"	3000	X	X	X	X	X	X		X	X	Yes
Rhode Island	60'	N/S	8'6"	13'6"	4000	X	X	X	X	X		X	X		N/S
South Carolina		53'[11]	8'6"	13'6"	3000	X	X	X	X	X	X		X		No
South Dakota	70'	53'	8'6"	14'	3000	X	X	X	X	X	X	X	X[4]		Yes
Tennessee	65'	50'	8'6"	13'6"	3000	X	X	X	X	X	X	X	X		No
Texas	55'	N/S	8'6"	13'6"	4500		X	X	X[6]	X	X	X	X[4]	X	Yes
Utah	65'	48'	8'6"	14'	2000	X	X	X	X[6]	X	X		X[4]	X	N/S
Vermont	60'	45'	8'6"	13'6"	3000[13]	X	X	X	X[6]	X		X	X	X	Yes
Virginia	60'	N/S	8'	13'6"	3000	X	X	X	X[12]	X	X	X	X	X	Yes
Washington	65'	48'	8'6"	14'	3000[13]	X	X	X	X[6]	X	X	X[6]	X[4]	X	Yes
West Virginia	55'	N/S	8'	13'6"	3000		X	X	X	X	X	X	X	X	No
Wisconsin	60'	40'	8'6"	13'6"	3000	X	X	X	X	X	X[6]			X	No
Wyoming	85'	60'	8'6"	14'	[7]		X	X		X	X		X[4]		Yes

1. If original equipment.
2. Over 80" wide.
3. Must hold for 15 minutes.
4. Over 3,000 pounds.
5. Over 5,000 pounds. If weight exceeds 5,000 pounds, must submit to safety inspection.
6. If over 80" wide.
7. Brakes not required. However, state law requires the tow vehicle and trailer(s) must be able to stop in 40 feet from speed of 20 mph.

8. Over 6,000 pounds.
9. Only on vehicles registered in Missouri.
10. On roads with 12-foot lanes only; otherwise 8-foot maximum.
11. On interstate and federally designated highways.
12. If over 7 feet high and 7 feet wide.
13. Or if trailer exceeds 40% of tow vehicle weight.
N/S Not specified.

Courtesy *Trailer Boats Magazine*

Trailer Tow Ratings for 1991 Cars

(Note A) Make and Model	Approx. Towing Vehicle Weight (lbs.) (note B)	4x4, Front or Rear Drive (note C)	Engine Size (note D)		Notes on Trailer Towing Extras Req'd.	Max Gross Trailer Weight/ Tongue Weight (lbs.) as Rated by Manufacturer (notes E, F)
			Displacement (liters)	No. of cyl & hp		
6 SMALL CARS (under 2,400 lbs. curb weight)						
Plymouth Colt	2,185	FWD	1.5	4/92	(2)	1,000/100
Ford Escort	2,287	FWD	1.9	4/88	(1, 2)	1,000/100
Nissan Sentra	2,340	FWD	1.6	4/70	None	1,000/100
Pontiac Le Mans	2,136	FWD	2.0	4/96	(1, 2, 4)	1,000/100
Toyota Corolla	2,390	FWD	1.6	4/102	None	1,500/150
Toyota Tercel	2,050	FWD	1.5	4/78	None	1,000/100
22 COMPACT CARS (under 2,900 lbs. curb weight and/or 126 hp)						
Acura Integra	2,549	FWD	1.8	4/130	None	1,000/100
Audi 80	2,844	FWD	2.3	5/130	(2, 3, 4)	1,235/110
Buick Skylark	2,625	FWD	2.3	4/160	(1, 2, 4)	1,000/100
Buick Century	2,769	FWD	3.3	V6/160	(1, 2, 4)	1,000/100
Chevy Cavalier	2,485	FWD	2.2	4/95	(1)	1,000/100
Chevy Beretta	2,655	FWD	2.2	4/95	(1, 2)	2,000/200
Chevy Lumina Sedan	3,192	FWD	2.5	4/105	None	1,000/100
Chrysler LeBaron	2,971	FWD	2.5	4/100	(2)	2,000/200
Dodge Shadow	2,708	FWD	2.5	4/100	None	2,000/200
Ford Mustang	2,759	RWD	2.3	4/98	(2, 4)	1,000/100
Ford Tempo	2,529	FWD	2.3	4/98	(2, 4)	1,000/100
Honda Accord	2,733	FWD	2.2	4/125	None	1,000/100
Honda Prelude	2,685	FWD	2.0	4/135	None	1,000/100
Hyundai Sonata	2,885	FWD	2.4	4/110	None	1,000/100
Nissan Stanza	2,905	FWD	2.0	4/94	None	1,000/100
Olds Cutlass Ciera	2,813	FWD	2.5	4/110	(1)	1,000/100
Peugeot 405 Wagon	2,690	FWD	1.9	4/110	(4)	1,345/135
Pontiac Sunbird	2,366	FWD	2.0	4/165	(1, 2, 4)	1,000/100
Pontiac Grand Am	2,492	FWD	2.3	4/160	(1, 2, 4)	1,000/100
Saab 900	2,760	FWD	2.1	4/140	(2, 4, 5)	2,000/200
Toyota Celica	2,747	RWD	2.2	4/130	None	2,000/200
Toyota Camry	2,745	FWD	2.0	4/115	None	2,000/200

Make and Model	Approx. Towing Vehicle Weight (lbs.) (note B)	4x4, Front or Rear Drive (note C)	Engine Size (note D)		Notes on Trailer Towing Extras Req'd.	Max Gross Trailer Weight/ Tongue Weight (lbs.) as Rated by Manufacturer (notes E, F)
			Displace- ment (liters)	No. of cyl & hp		
29 MEDIUM CARS (under 3,700 lbs. curb weight and 127 hp or more)						
Acura Legend	3,185	FWD	2.7	V6/161	None	1,000/100
Audi 90	2,999	FWD	2.3	5/130	(2, 3, 4)	1,279/110
Audi 100 (3)	3,153	FWD	2.3	5/130	(2, 3, 4)	1,455/110
Audi 200 & Quattro	3,252	FWD	2.2	5/162	(2, 3, 4)	1,455/165
Buick Century Wagon	2,905	FWD	3.3	V6/160	(1, 2, 4)	2,000/200
Buick Regal	3,311	FWD	3.8	V6/170	(1, 2, 4)	2,000/200
Buick Le Sabre	3,270	FWD	3.8	V6/165	(2, 4, 7)	2,000/200
Buick Park Ave	3,607	FWD	3.8	V6/165	(2, 4, 7)	3,000/300
Cadillac DeVille	3,466	FWD	4.5	V8/180	None	1,000/100
Cadillac Seville	3,479	FWD	4.5	V8/180	None	1,000/100
Chrysler Imperial	3,423	FWD	3.3	V6/147	(2)	2,000/200
Eagle Premier	3,031	FWD	3.0	V6/150	(1)	1,000/100
Ford Probe	2,730	FWD	2.2	4/145	(2)	1,500/150
Ford Taurus	3,049	FWD	3.0	V6/145	(2, 4)	2,000/200
Ford Thunderbird	3,550	RWD	3.8	V6/140	(1, 4)	2,000/200
Lincoln Continental	3,633	FWD	3.8	V6/155	(1, 2)	2,000/200
Nissan 300-ZX	3,219	RWD	3.0	V6/222	(4)	1,000/100
Nissan Maxima	3,150	FWD	3.0	V6/157	None	1,000/100
Olds Cutlass Supreme	3,286	FWD	3.1	V6/135	(1)	2,000/200
Olds 98	3,606	FWD	3.8	V6/170	(7)	3,000/300
Pontiac Bonneville	3,360	FWD	3.8	V6/150	(1, 2, 4)	2,000/200
Pontiac 6000	3,105	FWD	3.1	V8/135	(1, 2, 4)	2,000/200
Pontiac Grand Prix	3,038	FWD	2.3	4/150	(1, 2, 4)	1,000/100
Peugeot 505 Wagon	3,305	RWD	2.2	4/160	(4)	3,305/330
Saab 9000	3,100	FWD	2.3	4/150	(2, 4, 5)	2,000/165
Subaru Legacy	3,100	FWD/4x4	2.2	4/135	(4)	2,000/200
Toyota Cressida	3,335	RWD	3.0	6/232	None	2,000/200
Volvo 740 Turbo	3,177	RWD	2.3	4/162	(6)	3,300/110
Volvo 940 Turbo and SE	3,300	RWD	2.3	4/162	(6)	3,300/165
8 LARGE CARS (3,700 lbs. or greater curb weight)						
Buick Roadmstr Wgn.	4,415	RWD	5.0	V8/170	(2, 4, 7)	5,000/500
Cadillac Brougham	4,282	RWD	5.7	V8/175	(7)	5,000/500
Chevy Caprice V8	3,907	RWD	5.0	V8/170	(7)	5,000/600
Ford Crown Victoria	3,822	RWD	5.0	V8/150	(7)	5,000/750
Jaguar XJ6	3,903	RWD	4.0	6/223	(5, 9)	3,300/110

Make and Model	Approx. Towing Vehicle Weight (lbs.) (note B)	4x4, Front or Rear Drive (note C)	Engine Size (note D)		Notes on Trailer Towing Extras Req'd.	Max Gross Trailer Weight/ Tongue Weight (lbs.) as Rated by Manufacturer (notes E, F)
			Displacement (liters)	No. of cyl & hp		
Jaguar XJ-S	4,040	RWD	5.3	V12/262	(5, 9)	3,307/110
Lincoln Town Car	4,025	RWD	5.0	V8/150	(7)	5,000/750
Olds Custom Cruiser	4,435	RWD	5.0	V8/170	(7)	5,000/500

APPENDIX TWO-B.

Trailer Tow Ratings for 1991 Vans, SUVs and Pickups

Make and Model	Approx. Towing Vehicle Weight (lbs.)	Front or Rear Wheel Drive	Body Height x width (inches, rounded) (note G)	Engine Displacement (liters)	Notes on Trailer Towing Extras Req'd.	Max. Gross Trailer Weight/ Tongue Weight (lbs.) as Rated by Manufacturer
10 MINI-VANS (under 4,000 lbs. curb weight)						
Chevrolet Lumina APV	3,462	FWD	65 x 74	3.1	(1)	2,000/200
Chrysler Town & Cntry	3,963	FWD	65 x 72	3.3	(2, 7, 12)	2,250/337
Pontiac Trans Sport	3,553	FWD	66 x 74	3.1	(1)	2,000/200
Ford Aerostar	3,665	RWD	63 x 72	3.0	(7)	4,900/735
Dodge Caravan	3,434	FWD	65 x 70	3.0	(2, 7, 12)	3,100/465
Dodge Grand Caravan	3,717	FWD	65 x 70	3.0	(2, 7, 12)	2,900/440
Mazda MPV	3,644	RWD	68 x 72	3.0	(1)	4,500/450
Olds Silhouette	3,648	FWD	66 x 74	3.1	(2)	2,000/200
Toyota Previa	3,455	4x4	69 x 71	2.4	None	3,500/350
Volkswagen Vanagon	3,460	RWD & 4x4	76 x 73	2.1	(3)	1,320/165
4 FULL-SIZED VANS AND VAN/WAGONS (4,000 lbs. or greater curb weight)						
Chevrolet Astro	4,025	RWD	74 x 77	4.3	(7)	6,000/750
Chevrolet Sportvan	4,050	RWD	80 x 80	5.7	(7)	10,000/1,000
Dodge B350 Ram Wagon	4,900	RWD	81 x 80	5.9	(7)	8,600/1,000
Ford E-250 Club Wagon	4,750	RWD	84 x 80	7.5	(7)	10,000/1,000

Make and Model	Approx. Towing Vehicle Weight (lbs.)	Front or Rear Wheel Drive	Body Height x width (inches, rounded) (note G)	Engine Displacement (liters)	Notes on Trailer Towing Extras Req'd.	Max. Gross Trailer Weight/ Tongue Weight (lbs.) as Rated by Manufacturer	
13 SMALL SPORTS UTILITY VEHICLES (under 4,000 lbs. curb weight)							
Chevy S-10 Blazer	3,361	RWD	66 x 65	4.3	(7)	6,000/750	
Ford Explorer	3,681	RWD	68 x 70	4.0	(7)	5,700/570	
Geo Tracker	2,238	4x4	66 x 64	1.6	(1, 2)	1,000/100	
Isuzu Rodeo	3,575	RWD	66 x 67	3.1	None	3,500/350	
Isuzu Trooper S	3,755	RWD	72 x 65	2.8	None	3,500/350	
Jeep Cherokee 4x4	3,012	4x4	63 x 71	4.0	(2, 7)	5,000/750	
Mazda Navajo	3,886	RWD	68 x 70	4.0	(1)	5,000/500	
Mitsubishi Montero	3,814	RWD	66 x 74	3.0	(2)	4,000/400	
Nissan Pathfinder	3,735	4x4	66 x 67	3.0	(1, 4, 12)	3,500/350	
Olds Bravada	3,939	4x4	66 x 66	4.3	(2, 7)	5,500/550	
Suzuki Samurai	2,090	4x4	66 x 61	1.3	(1, 2)	1,000/100	
Suzuki Sidekick	2,650	4x4	66 x 64	1.6	(1, 2)	1,500/100	
Toyota 4Runner	3,760	4x4	66 x 67	2.4	(2)	3,500/350	
7 FULL-SIZED SPORTS UTILITY VEHICLES (4,000 lbs. or greater curb weight)							
Chevy Blazer	4,350	4x4	74 x 80	5.7	(2,7)	6,000/750	
Chevrolet Suburban	5,500	RWD	76 x 80	7.4	(7)	9,500/1,000	
Dodge Ramcharger	4,600	RWD	73 x 80	5.2	(7)	7,500/800	
Ford Bronco	4,430	4x4	74 x 79	5.0	(7)	7,800/1,000	
Jeep Grand Wagoneer	4,498	RWD	66 x 75	5.9	(2, 7)	5,000/750	
Range Rover	4,372	4x4	71 x 72	3.9	(10)	5,500/550	
Toyota Land Cruiser	4,597	4x4	72 x 75	4.0	(2, 11)	5,000/500	
10 COMPACT PICKUPS (under 3,400 lbs. curb weight)							
Chevrolet S-10	3,110	RWD	61 x 65	4.3	(7)	6,000/750	
Dodge Ram 50	3,200	FWD	61 x 65	2.4	(7)	3,500/350	
Ford Ranger	2,820	RWD	64 x 67	2.9	(7)	6,300/945	
Isuzu Pickup S	3,455	4x4	66 x 67	3.1	None	2,000/200	
Jeep Comanche	3,280	RWD	64 x 72	4.0	(4, 7)	5,000/750	(13)
Mazda B2600i	2,930	RWD	62 x 66	2.6	(4)	2,000/200	
Mitsubishi Mighty Max	2,285	RWD	59 x 65	2.4	(2, 4)	2,000/200	
Nissan M.T.	3,350	4x4	62 x 65	3.0	(1, 4)	3,500/350	
Nissan Longbed	3,140	RWD	65 x 62	3.0	(1, 4, 12)	5,000/500	
Toyota 1-Ton Pickup	2,760	RWD	61 x 67	3.0	(1, 4, 8, 12)	5,000/500	

Make and Model	Approx. Towing Vehicle Weight (lbs.)	Front or Rear Wheel Drive	Body Height x width (inches, rounded) (note G)	Engine Displace- ment (liters)	Notes on Trailer Towing Extras Req'd.	Max. Gross Trailer Weight/ Tongue Weight (lbs.) as Rated by Manufacturer
4 MID/FULL-SIZED PICKUPS (3,400 lbs. or greater curb weight)						
Chevy C-2500	5,800	RWD	71 x 77	5.7	(7)	9,000/1,000
Dodge Dakota	3,600	RWD	64 x 68	5.2	(7)	6,700/800
Dodge Ram 250	8,510	RWD	76 x 80	5.9	(7)	10,900/900
Ford F-250 HD 4x2	4,335	RWD	71 x 79	7.5	(7)	10,000/1,000

General Notes

A. *Completeness of tables.* The tables shown here are not all-inclusive, but an attempt has been made to include at least one version of each make and model for which a towing rating has been established. Makes and models examined include the following vehicles which the manufacturer recommends *not* be used for trailer towing. In addition, most (but not all) manufacturers advise against towing with convertibles, sports cars, or cars with turbo-equipped engines.

Vehicles not recommended for towing

- Acura NSX
- BMW — all models
- Buick Reatta, Riviera
- Cadillac Allante and Limousine
- Chevrolet Corvette
- Chrysler — all cars with turbochargers
- Dodge Colt Vista, Dodge Stealth
- Ford Festiva
- Geo — all models except Tracker
- Honda CRX, Honda Civic
- Hyundai Excel and Scoupe
- Isuzu Stylus, Impulse, Amigo
- Mazda — all models except MPV van, Navajo, and pickups
- Mercedes Benz — all models

- Mercury Tracer
- Mitsubishi Eclipse, Galant, 3000 GT, Mirage, Precis
- Oldsmobile Cutlass with 2.5L engine, Oldsmobile Calais with 2.5L engine
- Plymouth Colt Vista, Plymouth Laser
- Pontiac — all cars with turbochargers or certain engine types
- Saab — 900 Turbo SPG
- Subaru — all models of cars and trucks except Legacy.
- Suzuki Swift
- Toyota MR2
- VW — all models except Vanagon

B. Similar Models. Certain vehicle brands equipped with the same power and mechanical options are basically similar except for trim and accessories. For example, the Chevy Lumina is similar to the Olds Silhouette and the Pontiac Trans Sport; the Dodge Caravan is similar to Plymouth Voyager and the Chrysler Town & Country; the Dodge Colt is similar to the Plymouth Colt; the Ford LTD Crown Victoria is similar to the Mercury Grand Marquis; and the Ford Taurus is similar to Mercury Sable.

Curiously, however, rated towing capacity may not be equal among these look-alike vehicles. For example, for the model year 1990, the Plymouth Voyager was rated at 3,350 pounds, while the look-alike Dodge Caravan C/V was rated higher, at 4,000 pounds, and the Chrysler Town & Country was rated lower, at 2,500 pounds. Similarly, the Chevy Lumina and Olds Silhouette were both rated to pull 2,000 pounds in 1990, whereas their Pontiac sister, the Trans Sport, was rated at a mere 1,000 pounds. (For model year 1991, all these ratings differences in manufacturers' specs have been eliminated, except for that of the Chrysler Town & Country.) The moral: Check individual capacity ratings; assume nothing; insist on seeing printed specs, rather than taking the showroom salesman's word for it. In gathering this information, we were misinformed by sales and customer service people on at least five separate occasions.

C. Transmissions and Drives. Automatic transmission, when available, is assumed unless otherwise specified. Many manufacturers reduce rated towing capacity for vehicles supplied with manual transmissions or four-wheel drive. Vehicles with rear-wheel drive are generally rated higher for towing than similar vehicles with front-wheel drive.

D. Engine Size Ratings. Today most car makers rate their engine size (cylinder volume swept by the pistons) in terms of liters rather than cubic inches of displacement. One liter equals approximately 61 CID. So, for example, today's big "5 liter" engines are roughly equivalent to yesterday's 301 CID powerplants.

Where horsepower is given, it is maximum horsepower, which is often at high revs seldom achieved in normal driving. Thus liters of swept volume may be a better indicator of actual power available than horsepower.

E. Basis of Trailer Towing Weight Ratings. Unless otherwise specified, manufacturers' ratings of less than 2,000 pounds (i.e. capable of pulling Class I trailers) are for trailers without brakes; in some cases ratings may be higher if trailers are equipped with brakes. Note, however, that availability of Class I trailers with brakes may be limited, particularly in the lighter load ranges. Of the 50 states, 90% require trailer brakes only for loads of 3,000 pounds or more.

In most cases, rating is for the gross weight of trailer plus boat plus equipment on board, and does not include weight of passengers and luggage riding in the towing vehicle. However, in some cases weight may include payload in the towing vehicle (such as, for example, in the ratings for Chevrolet vans, SUVs, and pickups).

In addition, in some cases manufacturers (such as Jeep) choose to limit rated towing capacity by the vehicle's specified Maximum Gross Combined Weight Rating (GCWR).

F. Tongue Weight Ratings. Where tongue weight is not rated by manufacturer, one rule of thumb is to use 10 to 15% of loaded trailer weight as tongue load for conventional trailers and 25% of trailer weight for fifth-wheel trailers when attached to suitably equipped full-size pickup trucks.

G. Body Dimensions. Vans, SUVs, and pickup trucks are generally higher and wider than traditional passenger cars, and may exceed standard garage clearances. If you plan to park your new tow vehicle under a roof, check first to see if there is sufficient clearance at the entranceway.

Notes Applicable to
Specific Brands and Models

1. Only a few special items of equipment are needed for trailering use; for example, some models may require special axle ratios or auxiliary transmission coolers.

2. Manufacturer stipulates certain restrictions. These vary, but typically include limitations on speed, not using overdrive or fifth gear, driving only on reasonably level roads and in moderate temperatures, watching for engine overheating, frontal area of trailer less than a specific amount, etc.

3.   Towing capacity is 2,000 pounds for trailers with brakes.

4.   Trailer must have brakes for loads over 1,000 pounds.

5.   The only towing equipment required is towbar and lighting harness, to be provided by auto manufacturer.

6.   Volvo requires ATF cooler for 3,300-pound capacity; otherwise capacity is 2,000 pounds, 110 pounds' tongue load.

7.   Manufacturers' trailer towing package is required. Specific required or recommended accessories vary by manufacturer. For elements included in a typical package, see Chapter 5.

8.   Vehicle must have manual transmission for indicated rated towing capacity.

9.   Jaguar has permissible towing capacity of 4,188 pounds subject to an 8% gradient qualification.

10.   Range Rover has maximum capacity of 1,650 pounds at highway speeds for trailers without brakes, and of 2,200 pounds in off-road use for trailers with brakes. In "low range" (i.e. at low speeds), on-road capacity is 7,700 pounds.

11.   The Toyota Land Cruiser is normally rated to pull up to 3,500 pounds. However, it may tow up to 5,000 pounds when equipped with special oversize wheels and tires.

12.   Manufacturer recommends using a sway control for towed weights over 2,000 pounds. Sway control device must be compatible with trailer brake system.

13.   Data are for 1990 model year; no data available for 1991 model when book was typeset.

Product Source List

Air Lift
P.O. Box 80167
Lansing, MI 48908
800-248-0892
800-727-9009
Air suspension devices

Hitch-Align
7100 North Street, St. 103
Worthington, OH 43085
614-885-2514
Automatic hitch/coupler

Bendix Brakes
P.O. Box 4001
South Bend, IN 46634
219-237-2100
Brakes

Kelsey Hayes Co.
38481 Huron River Dr.
Romulus, MI 48174
313-941-2000
Brakes

Toledo Stamping Co.
P.O. Box 596
Toledo, OH 43693
419-382-3407
Brakes and actuators

Atwood Mobile Products
4750 Hiawatha Dr.
Rockford, IL 61101
815-877-7461
Brakes, couplers, other accessories

Dico Division
200 S.W. 16th St.
Des Moines, IA 50309
800-247-1781
Brakes, other accessories

Roeco Inc.
7200 Midway Rd.
Fort Worth, TX 76118
800-288-4601
Bearing protectors, jacks, dollies

Unique Functional Products
135 Sunshine Lane
San Marcos, CA 92069
619-744-1610
Bearing protectors, couplers, other accessories

Car Top Sailing Prod.
P.O. Box 532
Marlton, NJ 08053
Cartop carriers

Thule/Eldon Group America
1 Westchester Plaza
Elmsford, NY 10523
800-238-2388
Cartop carriers

Yakima Industries
P.O. Box 4899
Arcata, CA 95521
707-822-2908
Cartop carriers

Vannor Engineering
19061 174th Ave.
Spring Lake, MI 49456
616-846-8580
Disk brakes

Null Brake Systems
P.O. Box 9336
Huntington, WV 25704
304-429-4513
Disk brakes

Bosworth Company
195 Anthony St.
East Providence, RI 02914
401-438-8411
Electric winches

Powerwinch/Scott & Fetzer
810 Long Ave.
Bridgeport, CT 06607
203-384-8000
Electric winches

Cole Hersee Company
20 Old Colony Ave.
Boston, MA 02127
617-268-2100
Electric accessories

Auto-Hitch Inc.
P.O. Box 5044
Largo, FL 34649
813-539-6493
Hitch guide

Midwest Marine Dev.
1545 Newcastle Lane
Hoffman Estates, IL 60194
312-882-7272
Hitch lock system

Master Lock
P.O. Box 10367
Milwaukee, WI 53210
414-444-2800
Hitch locks

PullRite Trailer Tow Syst.
13790 East Jefferson Blvd.
Mishawaka, IN 46545
219-259-1520
Hitches

U-Haul International
2727 North Central Ave.
Phoenix, AZ 85004
602-263-6811
800-528-0361
Hitches and accessories

Da'Lan Inc.
68 Walker Rd.
Shirley, MA 01464
508-425-9585
Hitches and accessories

Draw-Tite Inc.
40500 Van Born Road
Canton, MI 48188
313-722-7800
Hitches and accessories

Eaz-Lift Towing Systems
1318 West Bristol
Elkhart, IN 46514
219-264-3103
800-634-8152
Hitches and accessories

Reese Products
P.O. Box 1706
Elkhart, IN 46515
800-359-5505
Hitches and accessories

Valley Industries
1313 South Stockton St.
Lodi, CA 95240
209-368-8881
Hitches and accessories

Reliable Tool & Machine
P.O. Box 757
Kendallville, IN 46755
219-347-4000
Hubs and brakes

Automatic Equipment Mfg.
One Mill Rd.
Pender, NE 68047
402-385-3051
Jacks and dollies

Dry Launch Light Co.
1113 Greenville Rd.
Livermore, CA 94550
415-443-3140
Lighting and accessories

Dyna Plastics
3221 Forge Rd.
Shreveport, LA 71109
318-635-3600
Lighting and accessories

Fulton Manufacturing Co.
P.O. Box 19903
Milwaukee, WI 53219
414-321-4810
Lighting, jacks, other acc.

Wesbar Corporation
P.O. Box 577
West Bend, WI 53095
414-334-2381
Lights, jacks, other acc.

Hopkins Mfg. Corp.
428 Plyton
Emporia, KS 66801
316-342-7320
Lite Mate electrical comp.

Overton's
P.O. Box 8228
Greenville, NC 27835
800-334-6541
Mail order accessories

J.C. Whitney & Co.
P.O. Box 8410
Chicago, IL 60680
312-431-6102
Mail order trailer parts

Northern
P.O. Box 1219
Brownsville, MN 55337
800-533-5545
Mail order trailer parts

Trailer Parts Internatl.
P.O. Box 520963
Miami, FL 33152
305-592-1879
800-346-6909
Mail order trailer parts

Flame Engineering
West Highway 4
La Crosse, KS 67548
913-222-2873
800-255-2469
Portable tongue dollies

Epco
423 7th
Prosser, WA 99350
509-786-2936
Tiedowns

Kevlok Products
P.O. Box 40020
Tucson, AZ 85717
602-881-2130
Tiedowns, clamps, other

Berkley Company
One Berkley Drive
Spirit Lake, IA 51360
712-336-1520
Tiedowns, safety cable

Indiana Mills & Mfg.
18881 US 31 North
Westfield, IN 46074
317-896-9531
Tiedowns, winch straps

Extend-A-Hitch
9613 Trumbell Ave SE
Albuquerque, NM 87123
505-292-8018
Tongue extensions

Henschen Industrial
522 North Main St.
Jackson Center, OH 45334
513-596-6125
800-262-AXLE
Torsion bar axles

Dexter Axle
222 Collins Ave.
Elkhart, IN 46515
219-295-1900
Torsion bar axles, other

Torax Division Reyncorp
P.O. Box 48
Muskego, WI 53150
Torsion bar suspension

UCF America, Inc.
1025 Busch Hwy.
Pennsauken, NJ 08110
609-488-1800
Torsion bar suspension

Leisure Components
16730 Gridley Rd.
Corritos, CA 90701
213-924-5763
Trailer accessories

Wefco Rubber Co.
1655 Euclid St.
Santa Monica, CA 90404
213-393-0303
Trailer rollers

Balco Company
P.O. Box 168
Ladysmith, WI 54848
715-532-5557
Trailers

Boyer Industries
460 West 12th Street
Erie, PA 16501
814-453-7176
Trailers

Calkins Mfg. Co.
P.O. Box 14527
Spokane, WA 99214
509-928-7420
Trailers

Continental Trailers
7270 NW 43rd St.
Miami, FL 33166
305-593-9367
Trailers

Cox Trailers
Highway 11, P.O. Box 338
Grifton, NC 28530
919-524-4111
Trailers

Cruise Master
503 S. Mercer St.
Pinconning, MI 48650
517-879-2411
800-624-5463
Trailers

Dixie Craft Trailers
P.O. Box 351
Eupora, MS 39744
601-258-3251
Trailers

E-Z Loader Boat Trlrs.
N. 717 Hamilton
Spokane, WA 99220
509-489-0181
800-541-1600
Trailers

Float-On Boat Trailers
3001 Industrial Ave., #3
Ft. Pierce, FL 34946
407-465-7420
Trailers

Gator Trailers
275 East Marie Ave.
West St. Paul, MN 55118
Trailers

Harding Trailer Co.
925 SE 14th Ave.
Cape Coral, FL 33990
813-574-3313
Trailers

Haul-Rite Trailers
P.O. Box 499
Camdenton, MO 65020
Trailers

Horizon Trailers
7100 NW 77th Ct.
Miami, FL 33166
305-591-1292
Trailers

Load Eaz Trailers
1425 Adams Rd.
Bensalem, PA 19020
Trailers

Load Rite Trailers
265 Lincoln Hwy.
Fairless Hills, PA 19030
215-949-0500
Trailers

Loadfast Trailers
1420 Meylert St.
Scranton, PA 18509
717-346-0705
Trailers

Long Trailers
Box 1
Tarboro, NC 27886
919-823-8104
Trailers

Magic Tilt Trailers
2161 Lions Club Rd.
Clearwater, FL 33516
813-535-5561
Trailers

Magnum Custom Trailer
P.O. Box 1209
Cedar Park, TX 78613
512-258-4101
800-6-MAGNUM
Trailers

Myco Trailers
2703 29th Ave. East
Bradenton, FL 34208
813-748-2397
Trailers

Rocket Trailer Co.
10600 NW South River Dr.
Medley, FL 33178
305-887-7396
Trailers

Shore Land'r Trailers
Box 235
Ida Grove, IA 51445
712-364-3365
Trailers

Shoreline Products
P.O. Box 848
Arlington, TX 76010
817-465-1351
800-873-6061
Trailers

Skipper B Trailer Co.
780 West Mansfield Hwy.
Kennedale, TX 76060
817-295-2203
Trailers

Spurgeon's Sailors Trailer
Route 3, P.O. Box 68
Stockton, MO 65785
417-276-5101
Trailers

Sweetwater Metal Prod.
Industrial Park Rd.
Sweetwater, TN 37874
615-337-3466
Trailers

Target Trailer
P.O. Box 520963
Miami, FL 33152
305-592-6613
800-346-6909
Trailers

Tee Nee Trailer
215 E. Indianola Ave.
Youngstown, OH 44507
216-782-3341
Trailers

Trail-Rite Boat Trailer
3100 West Central Ave.
Santa Ana, CA 92704
714-556-4540
Trailers

Triad Trailers
90 Danbury Rd.
New Milford, CT 06776
203-354-1146
Trailers

VIP Inc.
P.O. Box 232
Vivian, LA 71082
318-375-3241
Trailers

Vanson Trailers Inc.
1220 East Hunter St.
Santa Ana, CA 92705
714-371-2711
Trailers

Wallstrong Trailers
1400 West 260th St.
Harbor City, CA 90710
213-530-2740
Trailers

Boat Master Aluminum
Trailers
12301 Metro Pkwy.
Fort Myers, FL 33912
813-768-2292
Trailers (aluminum)

Crown Trailers
P.O. Box 1355
Highland City, FL 33846
813-682-3359
Trailers (aluminum)

Trailex, Inc.
P.O. Box 553
Canfield, OH 44406
216-533-6814
Trailers (aluminum)

Wright Brothers
1930 Losantiville Rd.
Cincinnati, OH 45237
513-731-2222
Trailers (lightweight)

Brooks Sales &
Engineering Inc.
P.O. Box 263
Chassell, MI 49916
906-482-7293
800-762-0374
**Trailers w/built-in
hoist**

SKF Industries Inc.
1100 First Ave.
King of Prussia, PA 19406
215-265-1900
Wheel bearings

City Machine & Wheel
1676 Commerce Drive
Stoe, OH 44224
216-688-7756
Wheels and hubs

Design Wheel & Hub
2225 Lee Drive
Akron, OH 44306
216-773-7873
Wheels and hubs

Dayton Walther Corp.
2800 East River Rd.
Dayton, OH 45401
513-296-3113
Wheels, axles, other

Superwinch Company
Danco Rd.
Putnam, CT 06260
203-928-7787
Winches

Shelby Industries
P.O. Box 308
Shelbyville, KY 40065
502-633-2040
**Winches, jacks,
accessories**

Dutton-Lainson Company
P.O. Box 729
Hastings, NE 68901
402-462-4141
**Winches, jacks, bearing
protectors**

Index